Joy Comes in the Mourning: Love Is Forever

James E. McReynolds, Ph.D.

Parson's Porch Books

www.parsonsporchbooks.com

Joy Comes in the Mourning: Love Is Forever
ISBN: Softcover 978-1-951472-37-5
Copyright © 2020 by James E. McReynolds

All rights reserved. No part of this book may be reproduced or transmitted in any form or by any means, electronic or mechanical, including photocopying, recording, or by any information storage and retrieval system, without permission in writing from the publisher.

Dedication

To what really matters—

Living forever in the Kingdom of Joy

Family

Friends

Those in the Next Place

David H. McReynolds
December 28, 1953-July 27, 2019

"He passed over, and all the trumpets sounded for him on the other side."— John Bunyan

Books by James McReynolds
Published by Parson's Porch Books

The Spirituality of Joy:
The Least Discussed Human Emotion

The Joy of Preaching:
Encountering Jesus Through the Word of God

Dancing with God:
A Theology of Joy

The Silence of the Church:
The Spiritual Struggle with Sexuality

The Spirit of Joy Church

Joy Comes in the Mourning:
Love Is Forever

Contents

Dedication 3

Books by James McReynolds 5

Foreword 9
   Dr. John Killinger

Introduction 13

Chapter One 16
   Remembering David as a Saint

Chapter Two 28
   Feeling Angry at God

Chapter Three 37
   Traveling Through the Fog

Chapter Four 42
   Helping the Fragile People

Chapter Five 52
   Choosing to Be Thankful

Chapter Six 58
   Embracing the Mysteries

Chapter Seven 67
   Accepting the Reality in Peace

Chapter Eight 79
   Joy Comes in the Mourning

Chapter Nine 87
    Working Through Forgiveness
Chapter Ten 95
    Igniting Hope
Chapter Eleven 103
    Moving Mountains by Faith
Chapter Twelve 109
    Healing Completely and Forever
Bibliography 122

Foreword
Dr. John Killinger

The famous Norman Vincent Peale, minister of New York's Marble Collegiate Church and author of *The Power of Positive Thinking*, one of the most influential books of the twentieth century, named James McReynolds "the Minister of Joy to the World. "In the more than fifty years I have known Jim, he has never failed to live up to that sobriquet. Somehow, he has always managed to find joy even in his times of heartbreak and difficulty.

It is hardly surprising that in this book, which is about the death of his brother David, he talks of joy in the mourning and how he has managed to keep going in spite of all the tears and anguish. There is nothing fake in this amazing attitude.

Of course, Jim grieves at the loss of his brother, but somehow, almost miraculously, he seems to find the other side of grief and is able to give a proper thanks for his joyful years with David.

"Christians," he says, "don't mourn the way others do." At least Jim doesn't, and he helps us find our own way in the darkness when a loved one has died, and we are no longer comforted by his or her presence.

He doesn't deny the hard, irresistible fact of grief. Indeed, he reminds us that Jesus himself wept when he learned that his friend Lazarus had passed away. If anyone ever had the faith and knowledge to see death in its proper perspective, surely it was Jesus, whom Christians proclaim as the Lord of both life and death. He obviously knew that he possessed the power to resurrect his friend, whose body had laid in the grave for four days, and that he would use that power to bring him back. Yet, in spite of what he knew, Jesus cried when he heard that his friend had gone. His weeping validated the sorrow we all know when a loved one is gone.

It is the same with us, writes Jim. As Christians, we believe in an afterlife, and that our deceased loved ones will live again. But we naturally pass through a period of grief and mourning, for our very nature will not allow us to do otherwise. Still, we know that death does not have the last word, and that our brothers and sisters, our parents and children and friends, will pass through this strange, mysterious barrier called death into a new and glorious life beyond. That is the secret, the gift, our faith. We can weep and yet rejoice.

Most of us would never think to connect the sense of joy with the hard, cruel fact of death. Yet Jim does. His continuing devotion to joy throughout his life of faith enables him to make the connection at once, immediately, even before the tears have dried on his face.

It is all based, he tells us, in his understanding of the deep mystery of God, a mystery beyond all reckoning, yet the controlling factor in all relationships both this side of and beyond the grave. All life is a gift, says Jim, and therefore should be lived thankfully and joyfully, with a rich and immeasurable sense of gratitude to the one who makes it possible.

Thus, when we experience the loss of someone dear to us, we can look beyond the dark and depressing sense of separation from that person to the fact of God's having gifted us with life, and to the additional fact of God's having a life of indescribable joy and celebration for our loved ones beyond the grave.

Trust Jim, the Apostle of Joy, to have such a word for us, wrenched from his own recent and dark experience of loss. How fortunate his many parishioners have been to sit at his feet and walk by his side in all the years of his ministry, and to have him interpret for them the rich equations that remain even when their loved ones have been taken away and their lives have been altered for the remaining of their existence in this life.

A few years ago, I lost my wife Anne after more than six decades of indescribably wonderful intimacy and togetherness. I have since remarried, this time to a beautiful woman named Gloria, who lost her dear husband Freddy after fifty-five years of wedded happiness. Gloria and I freely admit that we still have occasional moments of sadness and loss when we remember our first loves, even though our live have gone on and we have found joy and solace in our present marriage.

Reading Jim's remarkable book about discerning joy in the midst of our mourning has helped to disarm my own occasional moments of sadness. Now, when such a moment steals upon me without warning, I shall remember Jim's testimony about his holding onto joy even as he and his family were remembering his brother David's passing, and I shall be reminded to not be sorrowful or despondent.

Thank you, Jim. You have ministered to me as you have so many other people.

Introduction

David McReynolds realized that life on earth is a gift. I feel his presence every day. "Love Is Forever" was written on the cover where his funeral-life celebration on July 3 1, 2019 was held at Berry Highland Memorial in Knoxville, Tennessee. David had just written the foreword for my book, *The Spirit of Joy Church*.

Every human being will experience loss. The losses may include death, the loss of a church ministry or a secular job, a divorce, a chance in status. Loss is devastating. To find our way back to wholeness can appear to be impossible. In my own counseling role, there is joy in offering an inviting and gentle approach to grieving. I always keep about 25 copies of the little book, *Good Grief*, written by Granger Westberg, to give to those whom I do mourning with and offer the hope found in the Next Place.

Elisabeth Kubler Ross wrote *On Death and Dying*, gives five stages people go through in grief. She gave the theory that denial, anger, bargaining, depression, and acceptance. Bill Blevins, a gifted professor at Carson-Newman University, gives a helpful seminar on "It's Hard to Say Goodbye." Dr. Blevins notes that people experience differing symptoms of grief at different times. Blevins teaches that some patterns that are followed hamper the process.

Grief is done differently by every person. It is personal. My brother had been suffering for many years with cancers. Ignoring grief leads to numbers of coping problems. Grief comes because we love. We are not released from grief. Being rich or poor makes no difference. Being gifted and successful in life does not matter. All the 7.5 billion people living on earth today will know grief.

David's death and all my losses in life have been tender times. No other human can understand. Our brothers or sisters each grieve differently. Spouses grieve in differing ways throughout the world upon the death of their partner.

Because each loss is unique, we need to seek the help of a friend with gifts in grief counseling. When I went through my times of grieving, I sought someone who had had similar losses to help me through this dark journey. I could not handle recently losing my parents, losing my brother David, and losing feelings of worth, being insignificant, unloved, and unwanted by those with whom I wanted to continue sharing the joy of the Lord. One of the gifts David left was a thick book on the history of the McReynolds family. We are a part of everyone who lived with or without our genes. We will understand this in the Next Place.

We live in a fallen world. The shock of grief and loss overwhelm us beyond human capacities. I pray God uses this writing effort to give comfort to the comfortless. God can answer the unanswerable. God can give divine thoughts in suffering and pain that cannot be said in times of ease and comfort. We need to listen as God speaks to us. With our family I gave quiet support. When I preached my funeral sermon for David and the family, I did not pretend to have healing answers. I shared my own insufficiency and the insufficiency of my words.

Pain is painful. Grief is grievous. We are not the surgeon who can mend the wounds. The Great Physician is not me or you. As an introvert, most of my grieving is silent. Silent and listening companions brings healing and lasting comfort. A dying is not the time to offer unseasonable solutions. There are no easy answers to difficult questions.

Our strength comes from the joy of the Lord and bathes us in humility. We must focus our eyes on God. We lift up the suffering in humble prayer to the Ultimate Healer. Nobody can be transformed by our human blunders in our own strength and wisdom.

Walking with God through death requires faith. "Do you want to be healed?" We have to open our eyes beyond the suffering and trust Christ in this time when grief strikes us in our inner souls and infects our bones.

One of my Scottish ancestors, George McDonald, once said, "The Son of God suffered unto death, not that men might not suffer, but that their sufferings might be like his." Friends, we have faith and hope for comfort in these hard days.

Chapter One
Remembering David as a Saint

To enable our healing the funeral home gave us seeds for planting flowers as we grieved David's death. We lit candles. We carry his business cards. Good grief brings joy and peace as we get unstuck. Good grief helps us to let go. I heard a call to not cling or act desperate. Jesus said, "Let the dead bury the dead. But you go and proclaim the kingdom of God." Good grief helps us establish a new relationship with those who have completed their earthly life journey. Could there be anything more selfish than to have a loved one to come back and then, at some later date, have that child of God to die all over again?

No other loss in adult life is so neglected as the death of one's sibling. I was Unimpressed by the lists of books on a sibling's death, I viewed more books on losing a pet, as bad as that is, then losing a sibling. Our culture assumes that few adults have contact with their siblings.

Brothers and sisters influence each other's identity in fundamental ways.

Sibling rivalry requires little explanation. Just living together in the intimacy of family life places us in tension and aggression erupts when egos clash. Sibling relationships may be close and intimate, distant, or formal. The relationship may be evidence of attachment issues, loyalty, or lingering resentment. The death of a sibling means the loss of one who has common memories with you.

Childhood critical experiences as a part of family roots in your past are magnified. My brother experienced me as pleasant and supportive in events like graduations, marriages, renewals, and even family funerals. Time changes sibling relationships, as it does all others.

Good grief is to pay tribute and honor to the sibling often. Tell their story. Say their name. Reflect and give thanks to this important relationship as love is forever.

Before he died, I told David I loved him and to forgive anything that might have needed forgiveness. I told him that we both believed in the Next Place. In heaven David is completely healed and knows the incredible peace and joy that could not be described by mere words. David was not lost, but he has been found. Some will avoid saying, "David died." I know David is where our loving God says he is. I long for some kind of confirmation. That's just natural. One day right after I came home from the funeral, I was asking for some kind of confirmation. On my way home from church, a yellow butterfly flew to my shoe and stayed for about a minute.

Butterflies are messengers in answer to a prayer. I asked God to reveal the spiritual meaning of that yellow butterfly. I discovered that a yellow butterfly represents joy. When a yellow butterfly flies around us, it brings highest happiness. Seeing one means that something exciting and fun is on its way. They represent new life. If one actually lands on you, they are indicators of departed souls who are knowing peace in the afterlife. A yellow butterfly can denote love, the passion inside the hearts of lovers. They also symbolize new life, a transformation, and a soul in heaven.

I sensed that David was happy. Dreams have been part of my life, good and bad dreams. Visions of David tell me he is still my David. God is caring for him better than any of us, any of his many physicians, and God is enjoying him.

Knowing David is with God inspires me to as the old signs along Tennessee mountain roads said, "Prepare to meet thy God." I think of my own death and my priorities. When we know special people will greet us in heaven, our deaths will no longer frighten us. David and we will be saints in heaven. Our work on earth will soon be finished. Saints are those who are close to God even if they got kicked out or left the organized church or were even canonized by religious organizations. David prayed and felt our prayers. David read the Bible with us.

He kept loving his friends and family. David's real treasure is in heaven.

David's daughter Amy sang "Going Home" and grandson Paddy sang "Amazing Grace." David was a member of the Pride of the Southland Band at the University of Tennessee. Several ex-band members came to the funeral.

Music is associated with the joy of heaven. David might now be hearing music with harps, angels and saints singing with quiet violins and cellos, trumpets with perhaps a glorious rendering of "Rocky Top." Music soothes our souls in the kingdom now and in the next place. All sorrow is washed away. God feels so close. God might even be singing with you. One summer when I served at the Sunday School Board in Nashville, I enjoyed spending summers at Ridgecrest Conference Center in North Carolina near Asheville. Both David and his best friend Leonard received scholarships to a class Christian Music Workshop, where they got to compose hymns and got guidance from the Music Department, one of the 22 portfolios of the Sunday School Board of the Southern Baptist Convention. David could be singing, "I wish for you my friend the happiness that I've found," from "Pass It On."

Young college students served on the staff of Ridgecrest Baptist Assembly. National Student Ministry was always my favorite portfolio in my calling as a public relations specialist for the Sunday School Board.

David and Leonard shared their joy with the young staffers and enjoyed eating in the dining room. I am grateful for that happy time in my own life as I shared joy with beloved young people at Ridgecrest and the other centers in those Blue Ridge Mountains: Montreat, Christmount, the African American Zion, Lake Junaluska, and other spiritual assemblies.

I am so grateful for David and the time we shared. After the loss of a loved one, what remains are the years of memories created together in joy and love. The culmination of travels, experiences, and bonding moments are always on the videos of our minds forever.

The time of grieving is the occasion to embrace those memories while cherishing that time that we were able to spend together. The year before David died, our family enjoyed a reunion in a cabin in Townsend, Tennessee. That was the last time the McReynolds family was together before David's funeral in

Knoxville. That family intimacy is reflected in my many photos and stories which we can share with future generations.

Our life journeys provide memories, compassion, and much love. No one ever told us life would be fair, but that it would be a fulfilling joy. Concentrate on what you have. Everyone on earth has stories to share. Some stories and enriching and wonderful. Other stories are hurtful and bad. Some are really funny. Some are evil and sad. Some are interesting. Some are boring. Some become long and involved while others are short and sweet. Ask everyone to share a story about the one you are grieving. I learned much about my brother through the words of other people whose lives he touched. Hearing these stories warmed my soul.

David's life was shared with numerous videos, a basketball signed by Pat Summit and the national championships won by the University of Tennessee Lady Vols, his many awards.

I reflected on not only David's healing in the Next Place, but the reality that he was physically gone. We cannot now create new experiences. I reflected on what life was like with David just a phone call or an email away. We regret missing future experiences. How do you sing the sad songs of life? We cherish the years of life with David. And that matters.

The day David died the family gathered to help give him permission to go on to the Next Place. The treadmill of the world kept moving. His children, his wife Cindy, his family, and his friends will keep on the earthly journey.

All David's important appointments will be left unattended. He will go on no more trips to Civil War places and his work with those memories. He was buried in a Union uniform just like those in the military which he wore during many Civil War enactments. All David's negative emotions—fear, anxiety, anger, or guilt, even joy, will remain powerless. David's regrets will be assigned to his past where regrets go. As the motto for Texas A and M University reads, "There shall be no regrets." Those mysteries about life and death will be made clear as he experiences more love, joy, and peace that he could ever have imagined.

David's image as crafted by him and those who loved him will be left to

others to complete. All David's visions and plans will remain forever undone. His appointment calendar will be irrelevant. All the rejections and negative critics will be gone as these will cease to sting or capture David ever again. All of our setbacks and disappointments in life are minor in comparison to the joys and accomplishments.

Two places none of us will ever live are those in the past and those in the future. We are dead there. Maybe that is why so many people stumble along. There is an old proverb that says something like: "Look to this day, for it is life, for yesterday is but a dream and tomorrow but a vision, but today we will live."

Grief includes dealing with two basic questions. How shall we live? And "How can we be prepared for the certainty of death?" My visions of death have been shaped by glimpses of the death which I have experienced. I thank God for David and the time I got to share with this saint of God.

Wes Morgan, a retired pastor from Norcross, Georgia gave me permission to use his poetic essay, "The Continuing Presence of an Absence" in this book.

"A long-time friend recently died, and today my grief poured out in these words: Gone! Gone—not here! He is gone—but something is here. I can feel it in my heart—in my soul—my being. Gone? How can he be gone? He was just here a moment ago—a month ago—a year ago—gone? No! No! No!

"I live with this Presence—this continuing Presence of an Absence. This Presence which engulfs me with its Absence. I sense the Presence and I look—but see nothing. I sense the Presence and I listen—but hear nothing. I sense the Presence and I reach—but touch nothing. How long can this Presence of an Absence last? Forever—another day. Today—another day. Tomorrow—forever.

Now—a lifetime.

"I live with this Absence—this continuing Absence of a Presence last? Forever-another day. Today—another day. Tomorrow—forever. Now—a lifetime.

"Presence- Absence—Presence Absence—Absence-Presence-Absence-Presence all day long—every day—right now—then

Am I Present? Am I absent?"

David was on fire with enthusiasm. People enjoyed being around him to warm up with his fire for living. There was always something impressive about him. As a child he read every word of the Compton's Encyclopedia. David could win on any quiz show. He knew something about most any field. He could solve most crossword puzzles.

David possessed intellectual courage. He would consider most any thought or philosophy. David felt every feeling compassionately. He was properly disgusted by injustice. He was humble in making sacrifices or admitting his wrongs. David introduced friends and family to new things to enjoy. David's life journey revealed highest happiness and even higher love.

I always admired David's commitments to his wife Cindy and their four children. All his promises were made with love. He never expected anything from them. He and Cindy never lived in a contract marriage. Cindy was and is also a saint. She never lived for herself, but for David and the family.

I admired how they gave up so much for each other. Commitments organized his hours and days. His love and commitments were consistent. A few years back, David had made a promise to visit his oldest daughter Amy in Northern Ireland. He felt weak and sick, but he joyfully made his way. Our commitments build character. They transform into the wholesome people God created us to be.

Life is relational. Joy comes with regard for other people. David's life was enmeshed with affection and was crowned with joy. His trustworthy actions were widely admired. As outstanding men who radiate so much love his questions were not centered on "who am I," but rather, "Whose am I?" With such men ego loses its grip. He was free from selfishness. People like David have an interior of strong values that even the threat of death cannot prevail. With commitments and promises fulfilled, people can be calm and relaxed in your care. Joy comes on the far side of sacrificial service. We need this awareness for life to be a forever thanksgiving, solidarity, and communion. Honestly, David's troubles were more than most others. His deep wounds were absorbed in God's love. Wrongs are forgiven. Something mystical happens. Eternal joy burns with a bright and beautiful flame.

Comfort is found only in God. Words in the Old Testament (Job 42: 12) and the last book of the New Testament (Revelation 21:4-5) offer deep joy, "Behold, I am making all things new."

David was one of my best friends. We enjoyed sports, movies, and the outdoors. I sit and play back memories like I am in a movie. I admired him from the day he was born. Half of me seems to have gone away. My therapist described it as losing a limb. When somebody tells you that it gets better with time, don't listen. Wounds heal, but when one has lost an arm, we simply have to live with one arm. I am still learning to function normally without him just a phone call away.

Grief has no statute of limitations. There is no time limit to those dull aches in your heart that will not go away. I do pray this book can be used in any death or major loss. No other love is exactly like that of loving and being loved by a brother. And if you have been blessed to have a brother who was also your best friend, that love with the joy of the Lord will cover you during the best of times and will hold your hand through the worst.

A few years ago I found myself in Saint Elizabeth Medical Center with pneumonia and lungs spattered with deadly blood clots. For a couple of days,

I was going toward death's direction. A physician said, "God must have something for you to do. You have survived the twenty-to-one odds from medical statistics about blood clots."

I was taken with a frenzy of thankfulness. I blessed my Lord for being alive on my earthly journey in my body. I thought of previous times I had had a brush with death. I thought of the day my daughter Linda was born. Walker Knight, my journalist mentor, was with me when I was told that my wife was in labor. I had driven to Nashville Memorial Hospital, and the doctor said it would be a few days. I drove back to Ridgecrest Baptist

Conference Center where I had spent the summer writing and doing public relations tasks.

Walker offered me a ride in his private airplane. Walker and I shared similar views on the Baptist denomination. He was known for founding a new Baptist Global Press, as editor of Home Missions magazine, and the joys of salvation. We started in his plane over the Appalachian Mountains.

And in an alarming and fearful moment, his plane's engine spurted and quit. We both thought it was our last moment on earth. Somehow, a miracle happened, and we got to the Nashville airport. That brush with death awakened our thankful hearts. Do we need to almost die for us to experience the feeling of joy of this moment? Near death is not required for us to soothe in the wonderful warm bath of eternal thanks. Walker died recently at the age of 95.

Remembering courageous people like Walker Knight, Anne Killinger, David, and a host of others has enabled me to grow spiritually. Sharing in their lives is the fastest way to connect to the joy of being alive.

"Life will bring you pain all by itself. Your responsibility is to create joy."

~Milton Erickson, M.D.

Chapter Two
Feeling Angry at God

Grief and anger go hand in hand. The Psalmist wrote, "The Lord has heard the sound of my weeping. The Lord has heard my supplication; the Lord accepts my prayer." Psalm 6:8-9. Hand the anger and pain over to God.

When we grieve a loss, we will experience anger. Anger can cause feelings of resentment. Our rage and fury will not bring the loved one back. Anger adds to an already stressful time. At the beginning of our grief, anger can be a positive aid as we get through each day.

We are often told that it is inappropriate to express the emotion anger. Being angry with God is unthinkable. Hand God the anger. As we progress through the grief, anger brings with it negative thoughts and energies. Letting go of our anger gives us the opportunity to reconnect with our loved ones.

In our time on earth, we share intimate relationships with our family, with our partners, our good friends, and colleagues. Anger is sometimes directed to those we really love. To maintain the relationships that we desire, we name what we are angry about, deal with it, and move on. Holding back our anger or any other human emotion diminishes the joyous possibility of going deeper in soul connecting with anyone, including God. I went inside my church sanctuary and screamed, "Why did David have to die?" The joy of the Lord and peace came into my body.

I thought that after my last talk with David, a miracle might come. And I was shocked as the end of his life journey arrived. I was not prepared for the reality of his cold, lifeless body that didn't even look like my brother. As David requested, I preached a sermon that really was healing for me, just as writing this book is healing and assuring. His death caused me to identify and accept what was going on in my own life.

Later I asked God to help me feel my feelings. Our family traveled to David's house and shared our own feelings. Our family grief included joy that David was finding more joy in the Next Place than he had ever known. We shared feelings and thoughts of confusion, guilt, frustration, helplessness, abandonment, as we realized anger was not our problem but another gift from our Father. In the book, *Good Grief* Granger Westberg warns us that anger and resentment are not healthy. He writes that anger is a normal part of grief, and by God's grace it can be overcome. (Granger Westberg, *Good Grief*, Fortress Press, p. 50)

Angry outbursts generated during grieving makes us out of control, afraid, battered. It is healthy to be angry at this time comes from being confused as God fails to respond as we have expected. At first, anger protects from our sadness. Nourishing anger and bitterness by keeping them alive with our outbursts, our words and our actions. We water a plant of fruit or flowers, and it grows.

Give yourself permission to feel angry.

Sharing our thoughts and feelings helps us overcome all the negative and to heal. Realizing we were angry with God and that that was not wrong helped us not to transfer that anger to those who are just trying to help us. God was the only one who could heal us in our time of grief. Remember God already knows what is in our minds. We don't even have to say anything. It is appropriate to share the pain, the confusion, and the anger with God. We would not express or even whisper our thoughts to just anybody. God realizes the details of our raw and tender feelings. Hand over the anger at the feet of God.

The Word of God tells us that even Jesus expressed anger. The apostle Paul advised, "Be angry but sin not." When Jesus was dying, our Lord shouted, "My God, my God, why have you forsaken me?" Despite the circumstances of our loved one's death, the question that Jesus asks is our own . . . "Why?" David's death came after thousands of prayers for his healing. He certainly fought a good fight. Jesus cry and quotes from Scripture gives everyone permission to voice our anger and pain.

During funeral sermons, I often quote Job. Like David, Job was a faithful man of God, who had lost his home, his vocational calling, his wife, his home, and his children. In his anger and confusion, Job expressed himself honestly and against tradition. The Bible tells us that "in all this Job did not sin, nor did he charge God with doing anything wrong." In Job 38, God shares some of the most helpful words about himself. Job comes to realize that God has the love and the power to ease his pain and frustration. We know that "our thoughts are not God's thoughts, and nether are our ways God's ways."

Writing this book can help me and others deal with our regret, worry, and our anger will be defused. When I begin the process of writing another book, teaching or preaching or praying, I ask God to guide my words. I want to bring comfort to those who are grieving. "Comfort ye, comfort ye, says the Lord." God will whisper into our minds words that will give us comfort.

How can we measure the life of a person like David? What can I say to you my readers about confronting death? David's potential was limitless. His life will be lived by us, David's children and family who now share the gifts of music, lawyering, traveling, loving which David's generosity made possible. The lives of every one of those who made the journey to earthly existence through being born. Life is not measured by the number of years we live on earth. The answer is not what a person accomplished, the material accumulated, the degrees earned. David's real value was what he gave to other people. In my funeral thoughts, I conveyed what a giver David was. His work included serving on church boards and teaching the joy of Jesus to others. When he served as vice president of finance at Bergan Medical Center in Omaha, Nebraska, the nuns and the hospital leaders cited how much David loved people.

Christians do not mourn the way others do. Death is really a transition from life to life for believers. David said that he could feel the prayers. He expressed his thankfulness for the time between his terminal diagnosis and his death. His lifelong friends came to visit with him. He was happy to share what really matters in life. Of course, he was in emotional and physical pain. He expressed his joy from organizing the McReynolds reunion in the Smoky Mountains the year before his death. He often expressed his thanks for the days he lived after getting the terminal reality. David cherished his life, but he finally came to know that death would be a wonderful transition to a place of joy. He wondered how God could get the glory for his death. God really gets no glory for our death. God does not get the glory from death, but our Creator gets the glory out of our lives. Just days before David died, he wrote a tremendous forward in my book, The Spirit of Joy Church. He said that he knew me better than anyone else and he was honored by my asking him to write this unforgettable encouragement.

David gave much to charity and his church. He was pleased to give of his financial resources to help others. When his son Joseph decided to go to law school, David offered to pay the bills for him to study. He had no love for money.

He fully understood what success and money were good for in his life journey.

Imbedded in David's thoughts was that we have a better life on earth if we seek God. He was not just talking about life after death, but the joy of life here and now.

David echoed the words of his parents and mine in saying, "If one does not have God in life, you will have a miserable unhappy life." Our family's hopes for heaven made life so much happier. Our biological parents had died recently. David believed mom and dad and all friends and family were there. Even in the most secular settings, David said, "I have relied on Jesus as my Savior. I know where I am going." David was confident that God has all our affairs in God's hands. He allowed God to guide his life.

When I write of the joys of life, I write from my faith. All Christians rely on Something or someone none of us can see, touch, feel, hear, or smell that is beyond our senses in the realm of human existence. That's why we call it faith.

Anger is stored inside all of us. Anger management is always a part of grief groups.

Sometimes anger is openly expressed. The sharpest expression of anger is pushed under the surface. With the fear of losing our jobs, friends, spouses, or credentials. Thus, the anger continues as smoldering embers rather than a blazing fire. Psychiatric therapists point out that anger buries itself inside the subconscious mind.

Repressed anger damages the human spirit in many ways. It is a common cause of clinical depression. Harboring repressed anger causes an experience of being overwhelmed by both real and imaginary trouble. Joy will be hard to come by. Some professing Christians think in terms of rules and regulations that bring no ways for healing.

Repressed anger harms the spirit, and also it harms the body. There is little energy or concentration, exhaustion and sleeplessness. Our unconscious causes the nervous system to continue in fear, ready to fight. The body's head remains tense, hearts beat rapidly, muscles are taut, and the stomach tight. Anger aggravates arthritis. Anger blocks the human system causing congestion at one end or constipation at the other end.

Unfortunately, mourners use suicide, a permanent solution. People who call themselves nice or mature are not at ease expressing anger. We store it deep in cold storage. Anger can then be described as an uncomfortable, dispiriting, heavy, frozen lump.

With strong faith or no faith at all, mourners are actually turning their anger against God.

God does not always prevent others to hurt us or harm us, and that is painful and bewildering.

Buried under a traditional pious exterior, there is that concealed snake pit of seething, hissing rage at God.

Most people do everything they can to keep faith strong, to trust God. They are simply falling apart. They can't hold back the tears. Grief is filling every inch of body, mind, and soul.

The loss is a nightmare. Grief destroys peace and security. Christian faith assures us that God is close to the brokenhearted, but those in mourning feel lost, abandoned, hopeless. We who minister to them need to share a vision of what God has for them in the future. (Psalm 28:7)

It is so easy to become distracted, to focus on the losses. Joy will come again. (Zephaniah 3: 17)

Love is forever. Love will come to you in tangible ways.

God permits us to be angry at God. In the Old Testament, we read that Moses speaks his mind To the Lord in no uncertain thoughts. (Numbers 11:11-15) Writers expressed equally forthright words in the Psalms. (Psalm 88:13-14; 102:9-10)

Jonah, Elijah, and Job vented rage toward God. Jesus died at the hands of rage filled people. The promise we hold is that Jesus rose again, and he continues to love us.

Children of God quenched his physical life journey on earth but could never stop his eternal love.

Mourners feel so weak beyond any explanation. Collapse comes from the sheer weight of pain and suffering. They just cannot see that the Word says that all things work for good. (Romans 8:26) God's mercies never end. God's faithfulness is perfect, beyond understanding. (Lamentations 3:22-23)

Indifference is the opposite of love. Faithful mourners have not been indifferent from God.

We spent our energy and hope praying. David died in peace trusting God until the end. When we express anger at God, it is best to express it. God is gracious toward us as God absorbs the anger. The Browning Library at Baylor University in Waco, Texas houses the work of Scottish poet Robert Burns, "O that some

Power would give us the gift to see ourselves as others see us. It would free us from many a blunder."

Chapter Three
Traveling Through the Fog

One winter day in Nebraska, I drove to preach at the First Christian Church in Weeping Water. The weather was clear that morning. When we got out of worship, heavy snow was falling. And heavy fog sat in. Nobody could see more than a few feet ahead. That day many cars collided including a huge pileup in the village of Eagle and in Lincoln. I was confused, disoriented, could not see, afraid I would run over the middle line on the highway. Visibility was reduced to almost zero. I finally stopped as I saw about ten automobiles on the right side of the road parked under some trees. I pulled over with them and parked. Nearly an hour passed before I bravely, but foolishly got back onto the highway and into the dense fog.

In the fog of grief, we cannot see the way ahead. We just can't imagine what life will be like from now on. We desire the comfort of staying cocooned on our bed or locked in our home. If and when we dare venture outside, we feel disoriented.

The Oxford University professor and author, C. S. Lewis described these foggy feelings of grief. He wrote an insightful book, *A Grief Observed*. He used the medium of his book to vividly describe his grief. He documents his overwhelming grief when his wife Joy died after only four years of a happy marriage. Like my brother David, she had a long battle with cancer.

He experienced writing as therapeutic. He wrote under a pen name. Struggling to make sense to Joy's death, he remained depressed and in a fog. Seeking a friend for counseling, his assignment was to read his own book. When an author writes a book that has been inspired by God from one's depths, the author can read his books years later and marvel that he was the one who wrote it. Only after Lewis went to the Next Place, his publisher was allowed to identify Lewis as the author.

Lewis was surprised by his own grief. He found himself afraid, confused, in a fog, without ability to enjoy living. He described te common fog of grief. "There is a sort of invisible blanket between the world and me spread over everything as a vague sense of wrongness, of something amiss." (C. S. Lewis, *A Grief Observed*, page 35.)

In grief we don't know what we really want. When I retired after more than ten years of service for the First Christian Church in Weeping Water, I spun into grieving. What do I do now? My therapist helped me through this foggy time.

In grief we really cannot say what we want. This is common. The only thing we passionately want cannot now be returned to us. We have no idea what we want now. The past can never be recreated. Sometimes we just desire to be alone.

Some feel uncomfortable around us. We prefer to be in our homes, but our friends talking together, but not to us. We ride on through the fog of grief. I kept writing articles and books, preaching and teaching when invited, doing continuing education and conferences. I wondered what to do with all my books and sermons and scrapbooks on my world travels and ministries.

Science reveals to us that fog is simply a low-lying cloud or a thick midst. However, we are so disoriented and helpless trying to travel through fog. When we think of the foggy times, we trust that we do not have to drive alone. God is the God of the fog. From the time of creation, our Lord has made God visible. God was known by humanity by way of fog, clouds, and mists.

Leading people out of Egypt, a column of a foggy cloud and a fire was used. Without God mysterious in the fog, the people of Israel would not have had the joy of the Lord for strength to keep on. God spoke to a few chosen disciples in a bright, thick fog at the transfiguration of Jesus. (Matthew 17)

The fog of grief clouds our minds, and therefore we just don't think clearly. We try not to give in to our fear. When the cloud and fog fill our being, remember the words of the Bible and know God is with us.

In my communications by preaching, teaching, counseling, or writing, my favorite assurance is "the joy of the Lord is our strength." (Nehemiah 8:10)

But that hazy foggy feeling remains. Joy can enable us through the darkest times of our grief. I cannot tell you when the fog will lift. Grief is as individual as we are.

God assures us that every fog will lift. Sun shines again. Surprising joy returns.

With our typical winter weather in Nebraska, I try to keep aware of how to survive a physically thick fog. I know enough to slow down. Some of those who pass by me that foggy day were later in a dich or in an accident. Quick moves are difficult through fog. I always use low lights into the fog. Bright lights will not be helpful. I am fully aware that we cannot stop in the middle of the road. If we cannot see the yellow lines on the roadway, we must get off the road. Move forward slowly and carefully when we are in a physical or spiritual fog. Watch the white center line on your right side or the road, not just the middle yellow lines.

We might say that God is that white line. Never take your eyes away from God.

God will blow the mists away with holy breath.

Traveling past the fog involves finding a new identity in those mists of loss. The experience of losing my brother was similar to that of becoming a retired minister. We must begin again the process of living. It goes way back to when I was 12 years old at a summer youth camp wondering what my calling would be known. What kind of person do I want to be?

I had simply floated into a social and spiritual life finding that my gifts and opportunities came out of nowhere. People tell us they are uncomfortable being around us. I was expected to remain as I had been. Without the strength of the

Lord, none of us will become whole. We just scab over, but never are completely and forever healed. Life remains fogged up. We must choose to live again. Some actually prefer to exist in the fog. Being a helpless victim brings pleasure. They can now excuse any failure. They face no responsibilities. They cease to work. Some do not desire to ever be well. The slow and steady movement toward enjoying suffering comes and they do not know it. The fog hides the reality of the connection between grief and all the social ills of our time.

They use drink and substance to feel numb. They get divorced. They stay in a neurotic and emotional prison that has spiral from the time of trauma or grief.

The offer for the gift of the joy of salvation is no longer sought. I pray that those still living in the fog need to examine where they are, trapped by wanting to sit down in the grief and not wanting to get well.

Chapter Four
Helping the Fragile People

After David's death, I was looking at the ocean waves from my hotel balcony in Huntington Beach, California. The video in my mind caused me to think of David. Grief comes and goes no different than the waves do. Waves are a natural flow with no specific pattern. Just like grieving, there is an energy associated with the breaking of each wave. The water hits the beach forming a vacuum as waves retreat back into the ocean. When a storm surges, the wind will change the force of the waves causing them to be more powerful and turbulent.

The ocean waves reminded me of the ins and outs of grieving. Grief is so powerful that this life experience knocks us off our feet. Only when the water recedes and calms down can we stand back up.

As a pastor and a therapist, I often hear, "My parent just died. I don't know what to do." One older man made an incredibly helpful comment: "I am old. That means I've survived and many people I've known and loved did not. I've lost parents, grandparents, relatives, mentors, co-workers, neighbors, students, best friends, and many others. I wish I could say you get used to people dying. I never did. I don't want to. It tears a whole through me whenever somebody I love dies. And if the scars from the loss are deep, so was the love. Scars are proof of love. Scars are a testament to life. Gouging scars are ugly only to those who cannot see.

"Grief comes in waves. When the ship is first wrecked, you're drowning, with wreckage all around you. Everything reminds you of the beauty and the magnificence of the ship that was, but it exists no more. All you can do is float. You find some piece of the wreckage. You hang in for a while. Perhaps it is some physical thing. Maybe it's a happy memory or a photograph. Maybe it's another person who's also floating. You never know what will trigger your grief. It might be a song, a street intersection, a picture, the smell of a cup of coffee, and the waves come crashing. In between those waves, there is life.

When it washes over you, you know you will come out on the other side.

Soaking wet, sputtering, short of breath, still hanging on to some tiny piece of the wreckage, but you will come out.

"Take it from an old man. The waves never stop coming. You don't really want them to stop. If you are lucky, you'll have lots of scars from lots of loves. And you will experience more shipwrecks."

Eventually grievers set aside their time of mourning. Helping fragile people must be gentle and filled with care. Tears come with grief. Even Jesus shed tears at the death of his friend Lazarus. Whenever church youth met in a group, they were often asked to quote a verse from the Bible. I don't know about others, but in my youth times at Woodlawn Baptist Church in Bristol, Tennessee, more than once some would quote "Jesus wept." (John 1 1 :35) These two simple words record

Jesus' reaction as he approached Lazarus' tomb. This example shows that we need not be frustrated or embarrassed by our tears. Nobody will see it as a sign of weakness. Some are uncomfortable with tears because they grew up hearing parents say, "Grow up. Stop being a baby. Stop crying." We resist crying.

However, we cry because we love. We should never be ashamed to cry.

Tears can wash away our sadness, fear, and anxiety. Still we are surprised by the intensity of our feelings. Sorrow, stress, pain, anger, and even times of joy cause our tears to flow. During a sports event, both the winners and the losers are now crying for completely different and opposite reasons. It is impossible

to hold back tears in these rare and rewarding times. Tears are vital for our emotional well-being. Our tears bring us closer to God.

Reframe what you have learned. Give yourself permission to cry. Do not let fear keep you from embracing your tears. Visit the loved one's grave. As you drive in your car, imagine your loved one in the car with you. Say how much they are missed. Tell them you are happy they are in a place of joy and peace that is above imagination. Drive slowly and let your tears flow.

Allow yourself to cry. Tears release the tension of grief and make space for healing. To help you in this time be kind and patient with yourself. Express your emotions including the anger. Take care of yourself by eating nutritionally balanced meals. Walk around. Get some exercise. Write in a journal. To me I would rather write than talk. Avoid making big decisions or make significant changes. Talk about your sorrow with family and friends.

We are fragile and a healing support system helps. Many people will have trouble working through the natural process of grief. We know that life is fragile. To mourn is to live between the realms. Nothing is clear. Our fragile minds no longer understand anything about life. Everything we took for granted is a mystery to be unraveled. Answers are illusive. We may think that we can fix anything. We are just too fragile to fix anything when death comes.

When is it important to seek the help of other people?

Get help if your grief feels overwhelming or just too much to bear. You feel fragile and your emotional breakdown keeps going on.

Get help if you are having difficulty functioning at work, in relationships, or other areas of living life.

Get help if you continue to feel sad for three or more months.

Get help if you are experiencing physical symptoms such as body aches, stomach problems, difficulty sleeping, or always getting out of breath.

Get help if your anger is out of control. That can mean unfairly lashing out at others or behaving violently.

Get help if you have an urge to drink alcohol, eat too much, take drugs, or feel suicidal.

Get help if you engage sexual control problems or other risky behavior.

Not many of us have the finances or resources to withdraw from the world while we are in grief. There are responsibilities to meet, work to do, people to care about. The most important thing you can do is to take care of yourself. The grief process is a time for healing, deepening, growth, and ultimately transformation.

Grief is a time for rebuilding. As we work through the obligations and the grief, slowly give yourself permission to move ahead. Your loved ones live life on in your memory. As we enter this new cycle of life, we will realize that our willingness to recover and rebuild reflects the best of what our loved ones have given us.

Sadness comes as it springs its cruel surprise party. Death jumps out of unseen bushes or inside the clothes closet. Unrelated circumstances derail and devastate.

There is a thin line, an incomprehensibly small space between living and dying. The photo of David smiling and touching his great grandson on his death bed shows his gentle and quiet passing from this life into what is beyond. He breathed, then he didn't.

David would not want us to shy away from engaging and enjoying life. Perhaps we think of ourselves as survivors. We may think that because we continue to have the opportunity to enjoy life on earth, while our loved ones miss out on our times of joy. Nothing could be further from the truth. David lives with more happiness and joy than any of us who continue our journey.

David would want us all to be happy and experience joy. Permanent joy is being experienced in the Next Place as a crown of a flourishing and giving life. There is nothing wrong with our seeking happiness during our brief time on earth. We are given this one earth-bound journey as far as we know. David has surpassed happiness and now has pure joy. Happiness fades as we take for granted the things that caused us to be happy. Our deaths bring us into a joy that never fades away. We will be transformed. Love is forever.

Our earthly journey is fragile and fleeting. Life is a gift. There is no way we can know if we will live even one more day. Our connections with others add to this gift. Not one person belongs to us. Our gifts and possessions are fragile. God sometimes connects us to a new person who helps us discover hope. Love will guide us. We desire a sign to wear saying, "I just lost my brother. Please go easy on me and my family." Perhaps even if I had no such sign, I believe that if I did, it could cause those around me to give me space or speak softly or more carefully.

Our loved ones want us all to be happy. They want us to fall deeply in love, and to continue to enjoy new experiences. We who grieve can turn that limiting switch in our brain and realize it is the will of God and our loved one that we re-engage. Try to imagine if the roles were reversed. We would not want our loved one to stop living in that forever love that they now enjoy.

The fragile do not have a big sign on them, "I am fragile. Handle with care." Nobody has a label. They could be hanging by a thread. They work with you. They buy groceries where you buy them. They go to your church. Their children are enrolled in the same schools that your children get their learning. They reach out to the same doctors that you do.

Human beings are breakable, delicate, invaluable, so we must go easy as we encounter them. There are no signs, no proof, no indications of suffering.

Only when we can look with eyes filled with the strength of God can we see how to be in connection with their fragility. Life on earth is fragile. Human creatures are fragile. Handle them gently.

Dying brings another reminder that when facing the irreplaceable, irrevocable loss, all words fail. In the end, we can offer prayers and presence, to provide the kind of comfort that we wish words would. Simply being with those we care for and refraining from trying to speak allows more healing than any words that would be exchanged. And in those spiritual moments of silent presence the power of a better place will be felt.

In life we are surrounded by fragile people who are mourning the sudden passing of a loved one. They are wounded, pain-ravaged, and broken people stumbling into us. Most of the time we are oblivious to them.

No person has the tools or words for the fragile people. Sometimes all family and friends can do is "to just be there." We underestimate the value in "just being there." A voice inside us keeps urging us to do something. We think there is no effectiveness in presence. We need not bring anything. We are convinced that if we say the correct words, he will be doing the proper thing. Just being there is the most comforting gift we can give. In "just being there," we experience the griever's suffering. Showing compassion is a challenge. It is difficult to hang around in the long haul. We fear looking foolish or sounding stupid.

"Just being there" is holding a container of hope and affirmation which creates a vision for recovery. We can hope and believe for those in grief who are too fragile to continue the process to bring happiness and joy. It is devasting to struggle with their refusals of hope. One wants to run, but God helps us stay.

When complete healing finally arrives, they will be thankful for carrying the vessel of hope when there were holes in their own hope.

When fragile people try to deal with their grief, the emotions pour in like riding a seesaw. The reality of feelings toward one direction tips us one way. Helping us through grief requires a delicate balance between our old existence, and our new way of living. Friends and family stand with us as we discover the equilibrium where we can feel confident and comfortable. We think the old might be more desirable. The past relationships are now impossible to obtain without your loved one here.

Finding the balance between how life was and how it is requires an ability to re-establish the relationship. As we do this, we continue to merge life before and after our loved one goes to the Next Place.

We are who we are because of our relationship with those who were and are close to us and the experiences associated with our loss.

My lifetime friend John Killinger, whom I have had the honor of knowing more than half a century, and who has graciously written several forewords for my own books, shared an encouraging thought.

"The other day, I was having a bad time and I asked Anne for help. She died almost six years ago. A few minutes later, as I was driving down the highway, a car passed me, and I saw its license. It said LOVE AK. Anne's initials. I could hardly believe. But it continues to bless me."

If the only prayer you say in your whole life is "thank you," that would suffice.

~Meister Eckhart

Chapter Five
Choosing to Be Thankful

Life is a gift.

Nothing means more to those who are dying than relationships. The most meaning joys come with relationships. Our proudest moments are the times when we love well. Relationships give purpose and meaning to life. We are relational beings. There are no greater joys or higher levels of happiness to be experienced on our brief journeys to earth.

We can choose to be sad the rest of our lives. Or we can be thankful. In the beginning of grief, we think we have no control over our emotions. Any little reminder can result in tears. When we know healing has come, we can choose to be thankful. We choose to be in a spirit of thanksgiving for the life we shared.

It is the means to be surprised by joy. We grieve because we have loved and been loved. We will then mourn less the days we don't have. People of the joy of the kingdom of God are called to be grateful.

When Jesus healed ten lepers, only one thanked him. As you read about this, we can read into the fact that Jesus felt sad. He said, "Ten were healed. Where are the other nine? Has none but this foreigner returned to give thanks to God?" (Luke 17) Let us not be one of those nine who were not grateful that

God chose to heal them.

We are not called to be grateful for our loss, but we are called to be grateful in the occasion of our loss. Thanksgiving comes as we remember the story of our loved one. Telling the story is important. It helps us come to understand the reality and to accept it. This honors our loved ones. It helps us see the things for which we can be grateful. Only then can be peaceful again.

Life is a gift.

When we fully realize that everything belongs to God, we rejoice in how generously God has poured out showers of blessings. Fear of our futures will keep us from finding peace in the present time. We will then thank God that our loved one is happy beyond our imagination in the Next Place.

Those still on their earthly journey can benefit from the wisdom of those who have experienced death. They can teach us how when we confront our own deaths while we are still flourishing. We can remind ourselves that life is short, and every single day counts. The joy of the Lord is our strength to use courage, motivation, and faith to act on what we know is true.

Thanksgiving acknowledges the divine privilege to be alive and well.

God like any parent expects us to appreciate life's gifts with our gratitude on a regular basis. Wholeness comes with the spirit of thanksgiving. Thanksgiving tills the fertile ground for the eruption of miracles. In our complaining, we release evil upon ourselves.

The fruit of thanksgiving recounts the past, present, and future acts of God in our lives. With thanks we ascribe all glory to God. (Psalm 118:23) In thanksgiving, we preserve our blessings. (Psalm 28:5) Connecting with God in our prayers is not complete without thanksgiving. We thank God for God's good hand upon us. We thank the Lord for his perfection in all our concerns. In thanksgiving we do not stop bearing fruit in old age. (Psalm 92:14). Our thanks bring fruit in every age and stage of life. (Psalm 92:1-10) Thanksgiving offers a multiplication of grace. (Jeremiah 30: 19)

Corrie Ten Boom said, "Forgiveness is the key that unlocks the door of resentment and the handcuffs of hatred. It is a power that breaks the chains of bitterness and the shackles of selfishness." Forgiving a person who has hurt us or forgiving ourselves will free us. Unforgiveness causes nothing but pain. Until we forgive completely and forever, we miss out on joy and peace and love. Without forgiveness, we will keep doing a constant recycling of retaliation and resentment. David was a peaceful man. He exhibited a character to do unto others what God has done unto us. Forgiveness makes life more beautiful than anyone can imagine. As his family gave him permission to go home, David tasted the joy that he was completely forgiven forever. A soft breeze of grace blew gently across his face. He and we were thankful that he was made ready for his journey. David told us that his greatest joy was being alive. He wore a tee shirt with the words, "I'm not dead yet." He was grateful for the life he lived. David's hope for heaven gave him joy. However, he had learned to enjoy the blessings of this life. Of course, he could not help himself in mourning at least a little for the joys in life he would have to leave behind. What high happiness to have lived a life you hate to leave, even when you have a much greater place ahead. We can summarize earthly joy in two words: Being loved.

Our Visionquest for joy does not require that you make a long journey or save money. We are all surrounded by joy. David always thought joy was within reach.

He knew it had been with him all along.

David believed in eternal life. He knew he would live on after he finished his earthly journey. We live on in the lives we have touched. God is full of pride that God created David. David's life gave glory to God. We pay the ultimate homage to our Lord when we celebrate the life of one of his unique creations.

One day in my journal, I listed seven people that I was thankful for in my lifetime. I was amazed at that list. Not one of the seven had achieved success as the world defines it. Most of them were poor. None of them would be known to others. None had brought large gifts and changes in eyes of others. They were stars in my journey because of who they are instead of what they did.

In my journal each time I write, I write down ten things that reveal the grace of God. This stimulates my thankfulness and unleashes the joy of the Lord.

Releasing the past and forgiving everyone, including ourselves, begins the healing process. Unforgiveness brings on disease. Forgiveness is letting go. It is not condoning behavior. Each one was doing the best they could with the awareness, understanding, and knowledge they had at the time they hurt you.

Long held resentment eats away your body. Criticism as a permanent habit brings on arthritis. Guilt is self-punishment that creates suffering and pain. Forgiveness and resentment are the keys to our wholeness now. Physicians realize that humans bring on their own death.

Love, peace, and joy comes with appreciation of another person, beauty, our bodies, the joy of being alive, the process of the mind, and all things that lead to happiness.

Babies are naturally thankful. They do not do anything to make life perfect. They act like they know it. Babies ask for what they need or want. They don't hold back their emotions. They cry in anger. They smile in joy even when they are sleeping. Perhaps we all came from heaven. Intimations and memories of that joy still radiate from the days before birth. God tells us that he has known use even before we were born.

Babies die if there is no love. As we grow older in years, we accept the reality and learn to live without love. We all came with courage like that of a child. Fear overcomes the love. We listen to the fears expressed by our parents and those who communicate fear. We no longer love ourselves with that original spirit. We deny our magnificence. Jesus said we must come to him as a child. Children really know how to love themselves. We must go back to that time.

Thanksgiving and gratitude transcend any of our limitations. In gratitude, we recognize the magnificent and divinity that is inside us.

Giving thanks is positive and nourishing for our souls. There is no time to waste. Be kind to yourself. Be thankful for you just the way God made you.

Chapter Six
Embracing the Mysteries

Life is a gift.

Life is full of mysteries. Life is not a problem to be solved, but a mystery to be lived. Each step leads us into the unknown. Every single day we leave something behind, and we begin something new and unexpected.

I may never again visit my hometown. I had a passion to share joy in every nation and territory on earth. My mother used to tell me that I should never leave my home. When I left to serve as a student summer missionary with the Home Mission Board of the Southern Baptist Convention, mom said, "You can't do that." When I was at Baylor University in Waco, Texas, I was part of a revival team that traveled to Juarez, Mexico. It was my first international trip. David still possessed the Christmas gifts that I purchased in Mexico.

Why we go where we go and why we often do the impossible, or experience different joys and sorrows is a complete mystery. Grace comes with our blessings and our disappointments. This is really the story of every life. The mysteries of birth, life, and death overwhelm us. When we sincerely seek to become closer to God, our lives will begin mysteriously to lose our sorrows and become glorious again. We see the beauty reflected on us when storm clouds pass away.

When we are mourning, we find comfort in reviewing Jesus' brief years on earth. The mysteries of his life point to the joy of the Lord as our strength as we too add sunshine to others. Jesus rose from his death and went to heaven. God then sent the Holy Spirit to help us cope with life.

Do you believe so you can use your imagination to understand the mystery of what it is now like for our loved one to be living with Jesus our brother?

As I looked at David's bloated body, I tried to imagine what he looked like now. He now needs no wheelchair, oxygen mask, no pills for aches and pains. He will be ageless. David is radiant and glorious in God's love.

Think of others who need joy. Pray for those who are waiting for a baby to be born into our world. Do we need to share with those who need a job, money, food, or home shelter? The mysteries of life overwhelm us. We need to play those life videos of joy times in our minds. Soak up the light and feel of love. Find peace in picturing your beloved with God. Finish the work that God has given you on earth. Walk with God with courage and hope. Thank God for being with you through the mysteries that remain in our lives.

The apostle Paul wrote, "I have learned in whatsoever state I am in, therewith to be content." At least three circles of influence—you, other people, and life itself—interconnect in the same way one's personal influence affects those surrounding us. We need not feel alone in an uncaring world that throws troubles to us. There is a two-way relationship between life and each individual.

With Paul, we can become content with everything that happens. Our mourning comes as life keeps throwing curves. Until we embrace what shows up, we will not receive the benefits of lessons God is trying to teach us. We become tired and listless because we choose not to exercise our bodies. A blind man was brought by his friends to Jesus to be healed. They asked Jesus, "Rabbi, who sinned, this man or his parents, that he was born blind?" They were curious to learn why this curse had fallen on this man. And Jesus answered, "It was not that this man sinned, or his parents, but that the words of God might be manifest in him." Jesus was telling them to not look for why the suffering came, but to listen for what the suffering might teach them. We fail to understand that hardships can lead to us to be more loving, more caring, more patient, and more kind.

God gets glory out of our lives. David lived to pep people up. He lived for others, helping them along the road. He told me about a family who were in debt many thousands of dollars for health care at Fort Sanders Medical Center. As the chief financial officer, he found a way to write off all the debt. The Fort Sanders hospital system did not go under with such deeds of kindness.

In *Sound of Music*, Maria sang, "Somewhere in my youth or childhood,

I must have done something good." David said this in reflecting on the lives of his children, his nieces and nephews, his family. John, Joseph, Amy, and Rachel, he realized that in the mystery, he had done something good. He was proud of each one. It was always important that his life meant something.

Until the end with family around him saying it is time to go on to be with God, David focused on his blessing in this time of dying. His experience of dying was transformed. It was a new way that he viewed his entire life. "I guess that I have never realized how happy I am." Recognizing that his life had been full of happiness and joy, he looked on his approaching the end of life. We really do not know the mystery behind life, but we know it will be peaceful. David's cancer took his job and vocation away. He soon realized how much people loved him. The apostle James said, "Count it all joy." During the time of David's dying, we focused on how to live.

My friend Dr. John Killinger tells of a time when he was diagnosed by his dermatologist with malignant melanoma when a mole was removed from his chest. My brother David suffered for years with his malignant melanoma that led to his painful death. This dreaded form of cancer eats through the body, bone, tissue, everything.

Dr. Killinger thought about his dying. He feared leaving it all, his wife, his Children, his home, his ministry. John said that God mattered whether he lived or died. All must face death one day. In the mystery of life, it didn't matter whether he died that time or fifty years from now. John related how much he loved travel and adventure. He said, "Death is the greatest adventure there is.

It's like going to another country where no one you know has ever gone and come back to tell about it. Think how exciting that will be. Just trust God and enjoy it." John is still giving his life to make life better for all of us who know him. He is in his ninth decade of living.

John then expressed his faith: "I know you understand this, especially if you are older. We all live with death as we grow older. We feel it when it is harder to get out of an easy chair. We see it when we look in the mirror first thing in the morning. Death is drawing nearer and nearer. And the closer it comes, the more we know we need God. Only God answers the problem of dying."

Healing from grief is never easy. The mystery of life is not perceived with social mores and inbred value systems. Life continues as a mystery to be lived. Life is not ended with the death of a loved one. We are to continue to live and to grow. God never intends us to stop growing. It is a mystery as to why we face grief. Grief and death of your beloved person does not come from God as a punishment to you or me. God never parlays one life against another. God never takes one life to punish another life. It made sense to God that death was best. It is arrogance to think God takes a life to teach us a lesson. No other life is more important than the life of David or any other. That death did not happen so we could grow. Growth and maturity can come, and it comes much easier if we do not view death as punishment or as a sentence to a life of misery and loneliness.

We have more joy times ahead. We have more of the world to explore, new relationships to enjoy, and by living out the mystery of life, a new person can result. Our life ahead is still an uncharted mystery, but life is still a gift to live. There is one test for whether or not your purposed is finished. If you are alive, it is not done.

When I ask was determined a person's choice of a career, many have no idea. Some hope they can earn money. Some follow a parent, teacher, or one they have had much admiration. Those who do what their talents can enable spiritual joy and full physical and mental development.

Illness and death can result when a person retires. If a minister can 't create or serve as pastor of a parish, her insides are gnawed by the fire burning within. The decisive turning point among my retired friends is when they accept where they are in this moment. These times are difficult. Some do not have enough resources and money. Scripture reveals women and men seeking to accomplish the will of God. Biblical characters learned how to listen, what to say, where they could go, and what they could do. Those who have brought healing and life to others has broken the conventions of culture, even from the traditions of church people. Life mysteriously moves in cycles. There is time for us to be in a certain place. There were years when I used my talents like two sheets in the wind. I traveled everywhere. I limit the travel now. There is actually no such thing as retirement for any of us. Now as I approach the last decades of my life, I visualized my life differently. One day in my Disciples' Retiree Clergy

Group, we were asked to share what vocation we would have done if we had not given our lives to ministry. My passion is how to live in the later years. I treasure every surprise, every joy of being asked to serve. Within the work as Minister of Joy to the World, I am teaching my clergy friends to bring excellence to their colleagues to take their place as teachers of wisdom. Physicians say that all of us kill ourselves. God desires us to be healthy and vibrant until our last breath. Each moment of life can be enjoyed. Some remember my ministry see me as an old friend who helped them through confusing life events.

Deep in the center of my existence, there is a well full of the waters of love. I ask God to send me assurance that love will fill my heart, calm me, and radiate from me each day, the more love I give, the more I receive.

The supply of love is endless as my brother David knows as love is an expression of his complete inner joy. God has provided me with a comfortable home. I love me. I am doing what I enjoy doing using my gifts and graces. I use my energy with and for people whom I love and love me back. I attract loving men and women and children who mirror who I am. I have forgiven and released my past and all past experiences. I know that I could never create a new past. I am now free.

The deep mystery of God comforts us. Our minds by themselves cannot convince us of the mysterious love of God. Healing comes when we realize that there is a more effective way of life than the life we are living now.

God's joyful mysterious radiance has been with us now and forever.

The words Love Is Forever, printed on the funeral bulletin with David' s obituary has a deep meaning. We all cherish life and love. We must say yes to the mystery. In a later chapter, we attend to the power of love to move mountains. We become aware of this power, and a fire of love begins to bum.

Nobody lives long on this earthly journey without recording some unforgettable experiences. Not one of us travel the rugged roads of the world and the potholes. Where you live matters not. How much money or power you hold matters not. How much you love God matters not.

How careful you are matters not. How much faith you exercise matters not. How persistent and genuine are your prayers matters not. Hurt, pain, and heartache are unavoidable.

We still cannot comprehend the mysteries. Without seeing it coming, we smash into moments of loss and dizzying confusion. How we respond to these inevitable and unavoidable moments will unveil the mystery of how God allows life to happen. And thus, we are empowered to discover the secret to facing these moments with strength, grace, and what seems impossible . . . joy.

We are left with the mystery of what has happened. We want to know why. We have lost a part of ourselves that we cherish. The depression and pain become a lengthy grind and our energy wanes into hopelessness.

The mystery of why causes us to sit for years as we lose this treasure. There will be a piece of mystery that is left to just sit inside our souls, to tug and to struggle in us.

The trip will keep us humble by our inability to understand. We are in the middle of the mystery of life and reflect on the what and whys. Our inner eyes can scan this lost and found experience. Only then can we put this mystery away from us. God will give direction and guidance that gives us deep peace and harmony.

Only then can we live the mystery and enjoy the rest of our journey. John Killinger sums up the mystery in his prayer following a sermon on Psalm 23: "Whoever we are, O God, whatever our situations, you are our Shepherd. You have watched over us from before the day we were born. You will keep us until long after we have died. Fill us with a sense of your presence, In order that we may know there is a table set before us and see that our cups are overflowing. For yours is the Kingdom forever and ever. Amen."

Chapter Seven
Accepting the Reality in Peace

I have numerous scrapbooks of photos of my family, travels, and joys. Sometimes I marvel at how much people change. I have photos of hundreds of people being baptized by me and I rejoice again. Pictures of my family and friends from birth to death remind me that love is forever.

As I looked at my last photos of David, I saw his tired eyes, the painful small smile on his face, his frail body, I prepared for my tears to flow again. This time there were no more tears. I have accepted the reality with peace. Whispering to myself, I felt so happy that David was no longer suffering. As he departed from his earthly life, I accepted the fact at my brother was gone for now. I rejoiced that he is waiting for me and all his loved ones in a life that is heaven.

Grief is not an experience we get rid of like the flu. It becomes part of us. For most with faith, resources, and hope, it usually gets better. Our grief will never go away completely. We shall never forget our loved one and we will never forget our time of grief because of the loss. The hurt we will always remember the pain and the hurt.

Sometimes our grief comes back to us for a short time. We keep handing our grief over to God. His strength will lead us forward. We let go of those painful memories and become grateful for the good ones. Accepting the truth that we will never see our loved ones in this life, we rejoice that they are waiting for us on the other side of life.

As joy comes in the mourning, we hear God saying, "This is the way, walk in it." One morning I was revived and refreshed in my faith as I read Isaiah 30: 18-21. Read it as your dressing prayer in the mornings.

The disciples accepted the fact that Jesus was no longer with them in bodily form. They were filled with strength and hope. Not for a moment would they sit and mope in despair for the rest of their lives. When the Holy Spirit came on them at Pentecost, he inspired them to establish the church. Mountains were moved. The Holy Spirit brought a new reality with spiritual gifts and the assurance and inspiration to bring the joy of Jesus to the world. They saw what was real as they could now see what was being dropped before them. At a point in their grief journey, they had opened the doors to their souls and had no room for self-pity. They moved beyond their grief to move beyond grief into spreading the joy of salvation. The reality was that these servants would live a brief number of years. The twelve disciples and thousands of others gladly gave up their lives on earth. They died mostly at young ages. They did not waste one day. Their love and work filled the empty holes in their world.

Acceptance is the highest form of faith. If God leaves us in this world, it is because God has something for us to do. God's estimate of our usefulness is different from our perspective.

Acceptance of living is an important factor in healing. God's call is not the same for all people. Women and men with the enforced inaction in retirement often come to an early death.

Growing older means accepting that time passes. Customs change. Younger people behave differently. The older ones spend time with bitterness and criticism of younger music, passionate love, energy, and a much slower pace. If we try to preserve the beauties of the past, we will view faded flowers which cannot produce new ones.

Acceptance means accepting the sin of those who cause suffering.

God wants us to accept our fellow strugglers, colleagues, our place, and our nation.

Of course, in our day it is easy to choose a career wrongly. How many women and men who accept an appointment or a call from a search committee but work half-heartedly. They remain dissatisfied.

Fully accepting our life and work results in happiness, the solving of conflicts, victory over sin, and renewed vitality.

Circumstances do not cause us to be unhappy or happy. Joy and life are gifts. Fate is not to blame. Some eventually may come to being ruined. Acceptance is the only answer. The joy of the Lord is our strength. That joy transforms humankind. God can enable weak individuals to find energy, joy, and zeal in the battle for the defense of health. Health does not mean that we have no disease. Healthiness is a quality of life. This "abundant" life is a spiritual unfolding, personal dynamism, physical and mental wholeness.

If we refuse to accept death, we are stuck in a place where nothing appears the right thing. Thus, we have no direction, we continue to suffer. Faith and trust accepts that my brother David or any other soul will not come back. God requires us to open our eyes at the end of the tunnel. Seeing light at the end of the darkness, we honor God. Death is irrevocable. Humans tend to stay in that hole that they dug by themselves. Peace results from accepting reality and letting go of the sadness. Grief blocks the best memories. In grateful acceptance we remember the reunions, the good times, the early years, the joy and the love. These life videos cause us to smile.

Playing the negative tapes may cause those in grief to escape by withdrawing from the pressure of the real world. This appears in many subtle forms, preventing us from doing what we must do to improve our current circumstances. Fantasies come as we view ourselves as a totally separate entity from the one that is in an uncomfortable way. Even more emotional suffering is created in the moment we refuse to accept what is. Psychologists call this a defense mechanism. These defense mechanisms keep us stuck. Fantasy is not just wishful thinking. It brings on components that effect our lives here and now.

Without knowing the joy of the Lord as strength, we despair of solving the new vital problems. Concealing defeat leads to running away. This rejection of reality creates new problems that makes living more difficult. The flight is possibly unconscious. We use dreams. Real life is harsh. Life injures sensibilities. We escape the wounds by avoiding. Night dreams or daydreams are close at hand. Dreams take us far from painful reality. This takes much of mental and spiritual energy. We keep storing up secret treasures to turn the tables on reality. In fantasy, we play the star role, feels esteemed, seizes command.

Imagination can be healthy. The false images are sterile, ineffective, fatiguing, never restful or invigorating. It aggravates the wall between the ideal and the real. The inner soul is divided between the dream that is not lived and a reality he hates.

Regret and remorse show their ugly heads as we run maze-like in the past.

Others escape into the future. They are forever making plans trying to pull out of present pain. As an INFJ personality, I tend to live in the future. The only positive thing about this is that I can be a helpful visionary. Living in faith and joy means living in the present moment.

My older buddies take flights into the past. They are always looking backward, never forward. In a distant era, there was happiness and joy. Many people in the retirees' support group have accomplished amazing things. They served as pastors of highly desirable churches. They traveled the world. They savor the joys of the past.

While in Germany, I stayed at the Sleeping Beauty Castle in the fairy tale land near the Black Forest. The Brothers Grim were said to have composed their stories based on "once upon a time" and "happier ever after." Denial of reality brings the inability to heal. Fantasy is not related to the here and now. Fantasy is not being present in real life to what is happening now. We remain in a fog missing out on real life. In this state of mind, one ignores their own health, in light of the time of fantasy. Fantasy whispers in your ear for you to ignore reality.

We can pretend we are a Norman Rockwell family, and that nothing is missing.

Special courage is the only way to accept the reality of life as it is now.

In family therapy, there is always one person in the family who is the designated sick one. Their subconscious creates disease and functional disorders. Parents might have always been eager to be attentive the moment they became ill.

With an illness is was so much more pleasant than good health. They thirst for affection. Pretending illness gives a power punch. They avoid visits to unpleasant places, piano lessons, or doing a chore such as mowing the lawn or cleaning their room. The one who has been labeled "the sick one" suffers an inner struggle between drifted into fantasyland or to stop pretending. Being the center of the family becomes not what was desired. For nearly 10 years, I served as the chaplain and counselor at Valley Hope Treatment Centers in Lincoln and Omaha, Nebraska. I had also served those who were addicted to alcohol and substance abuse at Saint Joseph State Hospital in Missouri. Alcoholism is the foundation of mental health problems. Broadman Press in Nashville published my book, *Alcohol: America's Number One Drug Problem*. "More than half of all patients admitted to psychiatric facilities are alcoholics. Alcoholism is responsible for many other illnesses, accidents, deaths, and an escape from dealing with reality and freezing one's grief.

Alcoholism is a flight, a compensation for secret distress. Treatment that is effective must involve the whole person. The spiritual and psychological must be addressed. A woman who was a patient in the state hospital was finally going to be dismissed. The staff asked her what had helped her the most. She told them it was the worship services at Warach Chapel in Saint Joseph. One Sunday afternoon, I shared a message of love and joy. This woman was the only person who attended the service. She had been numbed with drugs, and I was quite sure that she never heard one word of my message. Yet that day, she told the nurses, doctors, and counselors that the worship during Sunday afternoons was the thing that turned her attitude and life around.

Escaping into alcohol is the same with other addictions. They are visible symptoms of personal soul problems such as shyness, idleness, distrust, inferiority, sexual difficulties, and weak wills. No treatment can bring freedom and forgiveness without spiritual work, without going back to the real causes of the addiction. Most addicts are not the drifters or the homeless. Many are victims of overindulgent and luxurious upbringing.

They isolate themselves morally and spiritually. Often, when confronted with the truths about themselves, they report that they are "spiritual but not religious." Give us a break, this escape into making the false gods an escape with their noble flights.

Some treatment center will not hire a therapist who is not a recovering alcoholic. Regulations insist that anything that hints of religious is not allowed.

The most dangerous flight is trying to escape into religion. Joining cults, intolerant religious organizations, or those who are the "nones." Their small mystic chapels become an island that cuts off the world and reality itself. They continue to wallow with passive pleasure that is pointless. These are the people who can use the intellectual sides of religion as an escape. Some escape with a religious conversion that requires no change, no repentance, nothing. Many go into religious vocations.

Feverish activity, political party pride, psychological escapes, outward demonstrations like falling on the floor, wild dancing, handling snakes, or continuous rounds of church meetings fill the spiritual emptiness.

Faith at its deepest is realistic. It is not a trench dug between dreams and reality. Inexhaustible religious activity becomes a sort of intemperance that blocks the road to healing.

During our time of grief, healing brings a respect for the Lover who goes through these sacred moments with us. Congratulate yourself for the courage to accept life as it is. My own therapist was another man who had retired and known grief. One thing he asked me to do was to write a letter to myself in which I wrote down my honest feelings and thoughts. How do we sing the sad songs of life? I wrote what I miss most about my life and those whom I have lost. By moving on in a loquacious manner, I keep my videos of joyful memories alive. We can now accept God's invitation to "live again," as Catherine Marshall said upon grieving the death of Peter Marshall, her husband who died much too soon. Some are given a long life and so many joy times to share. Most people live brief years in time. Acceptance of what is helps us to give up our human insistence that life should unfold in a certain way. Life after loss is overwhelming as we go from the pain to new visions, and we become at peace with the imperfections of life.

Accepting the reality brings healthier opportunities. We now see the barriers to joy swept away. Our life journey is truly a mystery to be lived. When our illusions are no more, we discover what really gives us strength. Peace comes as we accept the reality of the loss. Peace results in the presence of Christ in shimmering sacred spaces. If you are participating in a small group prayer meeting, remember the promise of Jesus that only two or three are needed. (Matthew 1 8:20, 28:20) David Livingstone, a missionary to Africa said,

"This is the word of a gentleman of the most sacred and strictest honor."

Speakers or writers who give the impression that they have a 100 per cent success rate cause me to be suspicious. Further investigation reveals lots of selectivity and wishful thinking in their reports. Honesty is absolutely required when we talk with God or other people.

We can expect surprises. Jesus continually surprised the people. Joy always comes as surprise. Jesus brought surprise when he stilled a storm at sea with just one word. (Luke 8:22-25) He brought a surprise by healing the mentally ill man who lived in a Gerasene graveyard. (Luke 8:26-39) The professional mourners who were called in to weep and wail at the funeral of Jairus' daughter experienced surprise when the little girl they were sure was dead, got up and walked around after Jesus healed her. (Mark 5:35-43)

Physical healing does not always happen. Many just a partial healing. Just as remarkable is a mental or spiritual change. The physical body gradually deteriorates, but with weakening bodies, the spirit gains strength. The body fades, the spirit shines. Joy comes as a blessing for the people around the one who is sick. Understanding, commitment, and faith when the opposite should be happening. Mysteriously, God uses a wretched and undesirable situation for God's loving purposes. God brings good out of evil. Accept the reality of surprises as healing happens with an attitude of flexible availability and openness to God. Prayer is never wasted as God is on our side.

We often say, "Why should this happen to me?" Phrase this reality in differing words, "If suffering is a reality in this world, why should I be exempt?" Becoming angry at God, we admit our helplessness and rage against our Creator. God accepts and bears our anger. My brother

David was confined to a wheelchair with his awesome pain. I saw a transformation in his spirit.

His personal Christian faith grew and deepened. His faith was renewed. He died a "healed death." His world benefited from his wisdom and courage in death, just as those who found joy from his wisdom and courage in life.

Nothing was wasted during his years of chronic illness. And with the joy of the Lord as my strength, I know David is with God, leaping and running and exploring life in eternity.

Unhampered by those disabilities that dogged his earthly journey, he is rejoicing in his heavenly home, where God will wipe away all our tears and death will be no more. (Revelation 20:4)

In our ministry, we look at God twice as much as we look into ourselves.

Mourning brings the joy that there is no person to whom the life of God is not there. Thank God for revealing that every person's life matters. In my mourning, I wait in silence as the Holy Spirit refreshes me. I am still knowing the purpose and the power of the kingdom is within me.

Concerning the peace of God, many think of this is something precarious which we must strive for or this peace will slip away. (Philippians 4: 7) We do not store up or keep the peace of God. The peace of God keeps us. Rest in the realty of that experience.

Peace is not a passive or weak time. Peace is an attribute of God. Enjoy God's peace.

God's peace flows all around you with warm, strong, life-giving fruit of the Spirit.

The joy of the Lord is our strength to bring others into the ring of peace. We share peace with others out of the peace that is within us. And God wills complete healing.

Our homes and churches are the places of peace. God's will is wholeness. As the Minister of Joy to the World, I experience the peace of God growing larger and larger.

Thanking God for each other, asking God's presence for those for whom we have been asked to pray.

The will of God will ultimately triumph. The peace will stay with us. The kingdom of God will come.

Chapter Eight
Joy Comes in the Mourning

Joy has been my life passion. I have studied it and share my concepts of joy in my preaching, teaching, counseling, newsletters, and all available media.

I have published more than 30 volumes on the psychology, spirituality, and fruits of joy. I have asked thousands of folks about a joy they have experienced. I enjoy people who radiate joy. Most of my six books published by Parsons Porch have been on aspects of joy. My publisher, Dr. David Tullock, sees publishing books as much of his ministry. He grew up as a Baptist. He attended the same school, Carson-Newman University in Jefferson City, Tennessee for his foundational studies, as I did.

My purpose in this book and other books is to show what a deeper and more joyful life looks like. I want to revolutionize the church by fulfilling my calling as the Minister of Joy to the World. I take no royalties from my books, but I hope Dr. Tullock can sell millions of copies. All profits from sales go to bring joy to the world by feeding people, paying their rent or bills that keep them in misery.

When we lock joy out of our lives for a long time, we must try to bring it back. When we ask God, joy will come running like a happy child and jump up into our arms. Joy might be experienced as a sly child, hiding in a corner. Some must make a unique and patient encouragement to accept the gift of life and joy. In my churches, especially the one located in Weeping Water, visitors came who had never heard preaching of joy. She said she drove around my church about ten times before she finally came inside the sanctuary. She had to be gently coaxed to trust us.

God does not desire that anyone live without joy. He created this world and the Next Place for joy. God wants us to experience joy in abundance. I extended an invitation to her many times. One day in her home, I read John 16:20-22 with her.

Less than a year later she died of agonizing lung cancer. God had given her time, her angels, and her church family to bring this time of grieving for her.

I baptized her and her family came to see her miracle demonstrated that day.

Seasons of suffering expose the deepest parts of ourselves. These times remind us who we really are. People traveling through the valley of grief are broken. They shrivel and shrink away in fear. Life becomes lonelier and sadder. To others, this sacred time makes them fully alive. Their new eyes see their personal and family visions differently. They may now realize that joy is real. Happiness is experienced despite our negative emotions as we reach toward personal goals. Life goes our way. Happiness comes with earthly success, some new ability attained, or a heightened sensual pleasure. In my life collections of descriptions of joy, I read of people transformed or a transcendence of themselves. Joy came on my daughter Linda's birthing a baby, our Ethan, into the world. Linda smiled as she gazed into Ethan's eyes.

Happiness is something we can create for ourselves. Joy seizes us in moments of surprise. Joy transforms us. Joy requires a spark of the divine. Joy is richer and fulfilling beyond happiness. Joy is dancing with God.

Joy brings a wholesome completeness, a revealing meaning, the most blissful moments. It comes in the present time and we feel fully alive in that moment. Happiness is pursued. Joy rises unexpectedly.

Joy comes early when we are involved in romantic love. Eating fried chicken by a creek, we glow at each other. As a man revealed, "When I make love to her, I just disappear." Sexuality and spiritually are entwined as A.J. Beaber writes and teaches with her work. This joy is a mystical attunement. This transcendent joy brings a oneness with God, nature, and all that is. Once we experience it, we want to know that feeling again, longing for that taste of eternity once more.

Flow continues as joy becomes more permanent as I visualize it in heaven. God now enjoys us in indescribable delight. Our joy turns outward to others. In a joy time, we want to tell somebody about it.

Grief and suffering bring new life. My brother David and our beloved now live in constant joy. They would not want us to continue to suffer. Their desire is for us to experience joy. David is trying to sprinkle the joy of the

Lord to us. Listen, pray, be aware of the little bits of joy that float around us.

Turning from grief to joy is a deliberate decision. God gives the gift of abundant life. Joy comes in the mourning. Jesus told us that the mourners are blessed and that they will find comfort. When we refuse joy, we impose a painful time upon ourselves. Do not block out the slightest glimmer of hope.

Soon after David died, I traveled to Huntington Beach. I used Psalm 95:1-4 as the theme for my Visionquest for Joy. It is always the first prayer on my lips.

It is communicated by millions around the earth.

As John Wesley said, "The world is my pulpit." He could only walk or ride a horse. We can drive, go on a bus, or by air to any place on earth.

The psalmist reminds us that we can seek joy from the mountains and also in the valleys. God is with us wherever we may travel. Jesus preached from the top of a mountain when he wanted to teach the joy of the Lord. Joy is that important.

When Jesus was transfigured, he was on a mountain. Jesus affirmed that mourners will be comforted. Our faith is tested at times of grief and sorrow.

So we can "consider it all joy."

Every person has had a share of hard moments. All we can do is cling to God and cry. Why should any be an exception. Jesus taught that choosing the "joy of the

Joy Comes in the Mourning

Lord" is possible, even in the toughest moments. We read with Paul, "Rejoice in the Lord always; again I say, rejoice." (Philippians 4:4.) How can people choose joy when they are in the fog while grieving?

Joy is a response to God's love and faithfulness toward us. Our joy comes from God. God's love never changes. Joy basks in the mysteries of God no matter what our circumstances are. When basements flood, houses drift down stream, lives and livelihoods are wiped out as with the recent floods in Nebraska.

As I coached grieving families who had lost everything, I suggested some practical strategies. One simple thing is to ask God for help. God delights when we ask our Lord to do divine willing and to "rejoice in the Lord." We cannot rejoice if we feel uncomfortable with hurting people.

I encouraged those in grief to count their blessings. Blessings were expressed. Sharing blessings brought peace to see beyond the pain. Just writing this book has helped me get past the grief. We all have people all around us needing to be encouraged so they can take their eyes off the present difficulties. Words are powerful. Send a prayer. Write a postcard, a text, an email.

Put those words into action. During the Nebraska flood, we helped each other clean, salvaged what was left. Cleaned up their family photos. Some made cookies. Others cooked meals for those who came to help in the cleaning of the mess. Faith shines in times of need.

Sometimes during our life, we may feel we are praying to a distant or unknown God. God invites us to come to know God as much as is possible.

God constantly sends symphony cards for us to draw closer to that joy. Each memory and every mysterious sign I become aware of becomes a gentle touch from God. What a blessing to have David in my life. I would rather go through grief than to see him in pain, suffering every day.

God seeks us in our mourning. God wants to wrap us in mercy. God delights in pulling us from our grief. We often spend unhealthy hours looking backwards. It is difficult to imagine our loved ones going home. My brothers and I felt like three orphans when our parents died. David's wife Cindy said a part of her had gone. From the Next Place, David whispers to us, "Open your heart to God's mercy. It is amazing."

In the highly acclaimed recent work, The Book of Joy: Lasting Happiness in a Changing World, Dalai Lama XIV wrote: "There is another Tibetan saying that it is actually the painful experiences that shine the light on the nature of happiness. They do this by bringing joyful experiences into sharp relief."

In my counseling office, I have a posture with a saying of Lao Tzu:

If you look to others for fulfillment,
  you will never be fulfilled.
If your happiness depends on money,
  you will never be happy with yourself.

Be content with what you have;
rejoice in the way things are.
When you realize there is nothing lacking,
the whole world belongs to you.

The ecstatic joy of being alive is within everyone's reach. Joy is bursting with delight.

Joy causes us to feel complete, grateful, and full. If we do not have the things we want, we can be grateful for those things we don't have that we do not want. We need to observe what has not befallen us to awaken to the joys of our ordinary lives. Beginning to tune in on the tiniest feelings of joy will soften us. Our essence, our souls will shine forth in all their brilliance and ebullience.

During my hours writing this book for you, I lost the first typescript on my computer. That was something for a writer to mourn. I use as much time as possible to preach, teach, and write. During journalism school, the professors emphasized that writing must be continuously exercised. Writing has always been easy for me, a gift. It is no more work for me to write a fresh sermon or an article or even a book, then it is for my brother, Edward W. McReynolds, M.D., to run a mile when he was doing iron man races and marathons. If I were to spend time on traveling to preach in distant churches, not writing anything, I would become less effective like a runner coming back to run after an injury. When my Apple computer failed to save my writing, I believed that I would just quit trying to write. Whatever is our calling in life, we must practice becoming joyous participants in the brief years we are allowed, thankful to do our part in the sheer pleasures of living.

Chapter Nine
Working Through Forgiveness

During our time of dying, we realize the bitterness, the anger, the grudges are a heavy burden that no person wants to take with them. Two things I always suggest in my coaching or counseling are first, to tell your loved ones to forgive you for any hurts you might have given. And second express your love. The last words David and I exchanged were, "I love you."

It was difficult for me and our family and friends to see David suffer.

He was stripped of his physical strength. We saw the pleading in his eyes.

This once strong man was feeble. He was a shell of what he had been. My brother had no fear of death. He expressed confidence that what lay ahead was so much better than it had been.

Death brings can bring numerous sorrows. The loss is complicated by other factors. Some people are still fighting an unfinished fight. David and I shared no such barriers. Some may be still carrying an unrelated anger that resurfaces in times of grief. We must solve each piece of our anger. I always felt calm and at peace whenever I was around David. We had a happy habit of always telling each other we loved one another. Grief is colored by who we are when we grieve and that special relationship with the one who has died.

Healing begins and ends with love. Love is filled with grace.

People who choose to be filled with "the joy of the Lord as our strength, "They have many times felt the release that comes with prayers and words of confession. Forgiveness is a gift, so we are not losing anything when we forgive and are forgiven. Unresolved guilt can cause us to live in misery. Guilt can be like the mafia of the mind. People often feel uncomfortable with a dying loved one. The most effective words David and I shared in the end was our assurance of forgiveness and love. Meditate on Ephesians 4:32 where Paul wrote, "Be kind to one another, compassionate, forgiving one another as God has forgiven you in Christ."

We may resent friends and strangers who were going about their lives without the burden of grief my family had. We must gracefully remember that this is not their turn to grieve. I experienced grief as I comforted my church members with my counseling, prayers, and funeral sermons upon their deaths.

Forgiveness may involve some unfinished business. In my prayers and quiet times, I talk with David, my parents, and departed friends. It is never too late to forgive or to be forgiven. Jesus forgave the criminal hanging on a cross. He forgave Peter for his denial. He forgave his disciples for running away.

Some things such as a medical malpractice, murder, or suicide seem almost impossible to forgive. Forgiveness is not a onetime experience. Rarely can some hurts and sins against us be forgiven and done with. It is hard to not keep on stirring up the videos of negativity and poison to our souls. Misery will not cease if we play that video over and over again. We must make a constant refusal to dwell on negativity. Serenity will not come if we do not let go. Jesus teaches that when a Christian has been hurt, abused, or slandered, the only weapon we have is paradoxical. This is forgiveness. Forgiveness has the power to free us from the harm of an unforgiving heart. Learning how to forgive transforms life in a spectacular way. Self-forgiveness is an important. If we fail to forgive ourselves, we cannot discover the way to forgive others. Humans tend to be ungracious and prickly, needing the joy of salvation that we acknowledge with gratitude that God forgave us, and we must follow God's lead. As God forgives us, it is presumptuous for us to fail to forgive ourselves.

Picture some hurtful situation from the past and invite Jesus to be there as we remember. As we allow Jesus to influence our thoughts and feelings, he will lead us to a new understanding and a new capacity for forgiveness.

We cannot receive forgiveness without a corresponding willingness to forgive. Forgiving and being forgiven are two sides to the same coin. Jesus' love is our resource. Our love is a response to his forgiveness. By his grace and saving power, when life has hurt us, we are able to respond with forgiveness. Forgiveness changes our lives. It is a healing path.

Grudges and regrets are barriers to living joyfully despite the pain. Forgiveness has a healing power. Pardon replaces pain with peace. Jesus talk of this in Luke 6:37 as he said, "Forgive and you will be forgiven." Grief is difficult to handle alone. Who can you trust? Trust those who have been standing by your side providing support before and since your loss of a loved one. If they did not care, they would not hang around during the most difficult times of grief. Fellow believes who live in joy care about your well-being. Nobody understands exactly what you are going through. Trust they will be honest as possible when helping you with personal challenges or just being your sounding board. Be cautious of those who you do not feel a connection. Trust your intuition and know that a person who radiates joy and glows with an inner light. These loving ones are not perfect. They have been through stress and exhaustion. Their commitments to live in joy despite circumstances are unshakable. They ooze serenity and it can't help flowing to you. Your instincts tell you these helps are not so spiritualized they cannot love the world. Those living in the highest happiness with times of joy are tied to a life of ultimate good. They have chosen joy. C.S. Lewis reflected this: "The load, or weight, or burden of my neighbor's glory shall be laid daily on my back, a load so heavy that only humility can carry it, and the backs of the proud will be broken."

Forgiveness is the core and essence of Christian faith. Only by God's grace and God's forgiving nature enables us to live with love. That faith translates into our willingness to forgive. Remember Jesus' story about the unforgiving servant. This servant owed the king more than he could pay in many lifetimes. The king began taking steps to sell the servant and his family into slavery. The servant threw himself on the king's mercy and that king forgave that huge debt.

That forgiven servant went to collect a debt owed to him by another servant. The debtor reacted by begging for mercy. That debt was just a few dollars, and yet this ungrateful man was insistent that he had to be paid immediately. He violated the other servant choking him by the throat. He then asked the authorities to put him into prison.

The story of this injustice reached the ears of the king. The king was furious. Jesus finished his story by saying, "In anger his master turned him over to the jailers to be tortured, until he should pay back all he owed." (Matthew 18:34.) In love, God forgives our sins, our own huge debts that we could never repay.

Throughout seven decades of preaching the joy of repentance that brings forgiveness, I have preached Jesus as the ultimate healer. I have watched painfully as unforgiveness continued to spread. Without repentance the untreated infections continue to spread. Forgiveness is God's way to set us free from infection resulting from our sin. Only the joy of the Lord can give us the strength to forgive. In our own weakness, we can never forgive. By failing to forgive just one person, unforgiveness will become your habit. That habit transforms our lives into negativity that becomes ingrained into your personality. Every sin controls a person by becoming a habit. If one fails to forgive the first time, that sin causes us to be less likely to forgive the second, third, or seventieth time. God knows that the more irreplaceable the loss, the deeper the wound, the more difficult it is to forgive. We cannot afford for those things to be fixed or replaced before we choose to forgive. Jesus taught us to continue to forgive others who seek forgiveness. Repeated forgiveness is the required command. (Luke 17:3-4)

In my calling centered on joy, my ministry is to show what kind of deeper and more joyful life looks like, step-by-step and in detail. My joyquests are about renewal and the joy of salvation that brings new wholeness. Carlyle Marney used to use the expression, "a priest at every elbow," to describe how we can help each other know joy. Open your souls to new stories of love and joy, stories of goodness and compassion, stories of peace and forgiveness. Cultivate a forgiving spirit.

Seeking forgiveness is an act of ultimate humility. We confess that we were wrong. Our forgiveness is giving up control and giving over the authority to another sister or brother to decide what they will do with your humility.

Until we change and choose the joy of salvation, we will keep on living with a dark cloud over our heads, wallowing in self-pity and hopelessness. When we shut others out, we forfeit affection, love, support, and comfort. Wading deeper into sin, we seek comf0l•t from harmful practices to find relief from the self-inflicted pain. We want our empty cup to be filled. That is why we turn to worthless alternatives.

Look into your own mirror and think about the hurts you have caused. Our own regrets may be so deep we have a difficult time forgiving ourselves. Every person has a story of serious blunders. Forgiveness of yourself brings contentment and peace for you and the people living in your own world. Thankfully, bad habits can be broken. We can choose to release ourselves into the persons God created us to be. The deepest wounds, the longtime of infection, and the desire for revenge can become so deep that it will take professional care. You cannot face this by yourself. Sin will bring thoughts of suicide, self-harm to yourself or other people. God will continue to encourage you to forgive.

God has an answer for all suffering, for all women, for all men, for every situation. Christian faith stresses forgiveness. We are to forgive those who never come to us in humility. Suffering is bound up with our disobedience and selfish modes of living. In the story of Jesus healing the paralytic, he said, "Your sins are forgiven." (Matthew 9:2)

There are no preconditions or requirements for us to forgive, regardless of others' lack of apologies or repentance. We do not have to wait for anything to choose to forgive. Sin cannot be undone. These can only be forgiven. Forgive others, not because they deserve forgiveness, but because you know you shall only live in peace as you do. What a joy to live lighthearted as you receive and give forgiveness to yourself and others. Unforgiveness toward yourself is still unforgiveness. Created in the image of God, we are worthy of complete and eternal forgiveness. That is why God sent Jesus to help us to be more like him.

Feelings of unworthiness disappear as you now joy in mercy and grace.

Forgiveness is a gift of compassion. God enjoys you. God delights in you. It is extremely difficult to forgive one who has jeopardized or ruined your life. You may have to forgive again and again. Jesus' strength can empower us to forgive once and forget it. He does not tell us to repeatedly forgive for one incident multiple times. Forgiveness removes the sin and cleans the wound.

We no longer focus on the person who wounded us, but on the consequences. The joy of salvation is that all has been forgiven. Forgiveness pours peace into your life. Now you're a fellow King and you become one with our brother Jesus. Your face will soften. Tenderness will sound in your voice.

As Minister of Joy to the World, I rejoice with people throughout the earth with all skin tones, all backgrounds found peace as they forgave.

Unforgiveness had snuffed out their fires of hope. Forgiveness reignited it. The joy of the Lord changed their lives. Life was still difficult. By God's grace their cups overflowed with joy and love.

Chapter Ten
Igniting Hope

How will we respond to the inevitable and unavoidable events? As we find the mystery to a heart of gratitude, we face life with strength, grace, and what may appear as impossible joy.

I can imagine David and us feeling the joy of heaven. All of us come by God's grace and forgiveness. We do not have to bring a box full of our unforgiven things.

At Christmas, David always enjoyed the movie *It's a Wonderful Life*. In the film Jimmy Stewart played George Bailey who got the opportunity to look back over his life and to see the impact he made on the lives of the people around him. In the end, the folks he had blessed were coming back and blessing him. The defining desire of David was the hope of the joy of the Next Place. The things on earth grew strangely dim. David moved from glory to glory from a good life to the best life. He knew that when he took his last breath, he would be in the presence of the Lord. That hope ignited all of us. We have many opinions regarding the words and phrases, or Bible verses we can use to express the transition from life on earth to our future existence.

Humans have always held the hope of living forever. The Egyptians tried to ensure a future life by creating mummies and placing earthly possessions for an afterlife. Spanish explorers searched far and wide for a fountain of youth. Baseball legend Ted Williams' family stored his body in liquid nitrogen. The hope of his family was that advances in the future would make it possible for the Red Sox slugger to be brought back to life. Scripture teaches about the inevitability of death. The writer of Hebrews wrote, "It is appointed for men to die once and after this comes the judgment." (Hebrews 9:27)

There is a sense that we do not belong in the world. With expectant hope and anticipated joy, we feel restless with this time on earth. Throughout history humankind has believed death is only a transition from life to life. With this hope for heaven we look around where death appears the most unavoidable fact of existence. When our thoughts turn toward heaven, we see the big picture. Death is puny compared to the vastness of life.

The opposite of hope is despair. To despair is just giving in. Trouble comes as we get stuck. We get bogged down in the mud as people are going to hell in a hand basket. It's easy to lose hope and to forget the bigger picture of a larger dimension to life. With a long view, we feel and see the signs and indications of the work of God unfolding. In hope we see our view is so much longer than one lifetime. Our hoping is no longer passive, but passionate in strong faith, we are part of the kingdom of God even now. Our hope is rooted in the life and death and resurrection of Jesus. Nothing else ignites hope. The Spirit of Joy Church is real. This igniting fire pulls us out of self-preoccupation and sulking. If we desire to experience the love of God, we must put our hope in Jesus. We must share what love means. The mission of those who have chosen to live in joy is to promote the hope of eternal living. We can believe that hope jumpstarts joy and is the leaven in time. What we do makes a difference. Joy multiplies joy as our gifts are used for the purposes of God beyond our wildest imaginations.

After prayer and determination, I feel optimistic about most things, such as job interviews. Nervous! Oh, yes! My devotion to work and life give me confidence. My past mistakes cause me to be cautious. Following David's death, suddenly in my journal, I wrote line after line, starting with, "I hope." Hope requires effort and strength from inside. Negatives thoughts and emotions will surface like bad limiting habits. (Romans 5:3-5)

Grief brings grace to view our pain as a method in which we grow. Hope helps us walk that holy path. This grace leads our weary souls to the wellspring of eternal life. Learning how to live joyfully when living becomes painful is our choice. Hope guides us through the work of change that has a lasting impact on the rest of your life. As we walk this difficult path, we need truth to speak louder

than the lies of despair. Hope comes in community as we walk through dark valleys. Companions who have walked before us bring hope. Friends hold our hands in the shadows with a lantern glowing as we move forward together. God brings us to carry our own mat to Jesus when we are powerless to take one more step. Every journey begins with a first step. No matter how dark these days are, or how wild our storms become, or how deep your valley is, or how long your winter lasts, there is hope.

One of my most effective questions I use in coaching is, "What would make things turn out alright?" This a question about hope. It is digging for where new life is found. Hope is different from a wish. Hope implies a relationship. We do not have to go through this by ourselves. As we experience the acceptance and love of other people. Love alone will not cure us, but love makes us whole. Love brings the promise of a deeper and new way of being related to the ultimate truths of life. The hope of the Next Place is that we will experience glory. David found hope as he gave himself away. People of hope are making a transition. David spoke with a child-like intimacy. "When I take my last breath, I'll be in the presence of One who loves me best," David said.

I spend quite a bit of time preparing funerals. I have officiated in more than one thousand funerals. Most pastors enjoy doing weddings, but dread funerals.

Funerals are gatherings of raw authenticity. The death of a loved one strips us bare and leaves us broken, yet beautifully open to words of hope. Death drives us into a vulnerable realness in a way that matrimony fails to accomplish. Life is precious. Love is forever. That is why I value funerals and feel it a privilege to lead, being graced at the opportunity to honor someone I have loved.

In our day, people just refuse to be uncomfortable. They refuse to make a conscious decision not to be sad, pained, or any unpleasantness. It is common to abandon any organized service. Funerals are sad. They are predicated on grief and loss, and some folks just have no tolerance for such feelings. They might sign their names at the visitation but do not go to the actual worship service. The word "funeral" means "rites for the burial of the dead." Some funerals are utterly cold and impersonal, the whole thing rang empty, dull, and flat.

Hope comes as we are assured that we will overcome this. Sometimes words, our sermons, our prayers, and our books plant a seed of hope. Pain does not have the final statement. If you choose, you can heal your life. Simple seeds of hope give the bereaved vital help. Remind people of the strength that God's joy gives. People radiate sheer joy as through hope, they become their best selves with some understanding of God's presence and his purpose and ultimate plan with implications of forever love and eternal life.

Death has the power to change dreams. It takes away our innocence.

Loss changes us forever. Going on is a choice. But the next coping skills are not just accepting our fate. Finally, hope arrives, and a mysterious miracle happens. Hurt stays for shorter and shorter times.

Those who shared the radiation of love will give out love again.

We cannot restore life, but we can find hope in the words of those who genuinely love us and be the facilitator for the bereaved to accept life for herself. God brings hope unencumbered by the noise, the sounds that clutter souls, and fill our days. Hope is found in the quiet, stripped-away places where God whispers love.

Grief does not leave you. You leave grief. We can dream new dreams. We will find the keys to open the door to more abundant life. Together we create an atmosphere for those who grieve to look within. If you come to know God, nothing has the power to defeat you. Grief can result in a deep and abiding faith.

Every human on earth will lose the presence of those we love. Love is forever. Today is the day to plant seeds of strength and hope. Mark Twain wrote, "Give every day the chance to become the most beautiful day of your life." We do not have to take each day all at once. One breath, one moment, one trusting step is enough. Only in that day can we slow down, breath, and accept what God has allowed in our journey. The hottest fire refines the purest gold.

Turn your mourning into dancing. Ralph Waldo Emerson advised, "Even in the mud and scum of things, something always, always sings."

There is no way to undo death. We cannot restore what has left the earthly experience. Death challenges our beliefs. Death taunts our hope. Life is jarred into a quick perspective. Death throws us off balance. We breathe reluctantly s we think we could drown in grief. Faith brings hope to strengthen during loss. We can gather under the wings of healing hope. Hope assures us that our loved one is now at peace. Hope does not spare us of the process of grieving. We are assured that we can and must go on. We realize that there will come better days.

Hope help as we let go. Listen closely to Jesus, and we will hear urge us to value what is still good in life. We are not to forget what is beyond this life. God wants us to invest in love. Letting go is the core of our healing. Clinging to the past only delays healing in the present. Life will not be as it once was. This will not happen immediately. Take the gift of time and patience. The final healing cannot happen if we stay in the way.

Now, every time I witness a strong person, I want to know: What darkness did you conquer in your story? Mountains do not rise without earthquakes.

~Katherine MacKenett

Chapter Eleven
Moving Mountains by Faith

Faith is the only explanation of how we get through any loss. We realize that We would never have had the strength to do what we did without the grace of God and the support of faithful people and prayers. Our family felt the power of prayer working in our lives. Not only does faith help us through the time of death, but faith nevertheless is challenged by death.

Faith is not a feeling. Many refrain all their lives from making any profession of faith. They take no part in anything that hints of religion. They never become enthusiastic. They never reach the conclusion that true faith does not consist of flights of fantasy, but faith includes concrete experiences. The realization for reality does not include God. They remain deaf to the call of God.

Faith is not something we either have or don't have. Faith is trust. Faith is something we do rather than something we have. Faith nudges us to action rather than squeezing back into fears and repeating things that have never worked. Jesus is the model for knowing who God is. He shows what means to have faith. If nothing can separate us from the love of God, then everything links us to God. To trust God is to not need proof. All life is a mystery to be lived. Uncertainty and doubt are at the core of human existence. Live in faith and know that God's ways are not our ways. God's thoughts are not our thoughts.

One of those professing faith in Jesus said, "I'd rather die forever following Jesus and what he believed Jesus than to live forever as one who turns away from him." With that faith the world is less shaky. Longing for life after death is placed inside every human. Grief intensifies that longing. What we believe about the Next Place is founded on what Jesus said and showed us about God. Even if life on earth was painfully filled, our hope is that God will resurrect us to something else. Everyone has some unfulfilled longings for life. That struggle is a part of our grief.

In that struggle we realize we never would have had the strength to do what we did without the grace of God. Human temptation to abandon God is natural. Even Jesus disciples had a feeling of abandonment. Jesus never said life could be lived without darkness, but he did promise he would lead us out of the dark. Getting free from the darkness results in seeing the beauty of God's love.

When we are having trouble finding God during our grief, we remember to be still. In this grieving, we hear much noise. We keep ourselves busy. We listen to the radio or television or constantly make use of the internet. We avoid quietness at any cost. In the silence we find God.

We read where Elijah learned this while waiting for God. He was on a mountaintop. He felt strong wind, an earthquake, and raging fire. God was not revealed in any of these. God spoke to him in a light gentle sound that brushed by Elijah's heart. (I Kings 19:11-13.) This might well be our own experience. We may not discover God at the funeral nor in all the noise of dying and death.

If we can become calm and quiet, we will encounter the spirit of God.

The writers of Scripture make this promise. (Psalm 34: 1 1-19; Psalm 46:2; Il Chronicles 15:20 God is sitting quietly and patiently waiting for us to open our door to love. If we keep our souls locked up, we cannot connect with God. The most amazing mysterious power is waiting. The light of God's love delights in washing all the gloom and darkness away. Reading Scripture, prayer, and silence will build mountain moving faith.

We do not need an extensive prayer. We just need to respond with a simple whispering prayer.

Faith is much more than just believing there is a God. Faith has confidence to do the impossible. Even tiny faith such as a mustard seed can move mountains. (Matthew 17:20.)

Mountains are moved one rock at a time. With faith, we can begin the moving of any mountain. This is so much more effective than sitting in despair and staring at the same old mountain for the rest of our lives.

God will not move the mountain for us. James warned that faith is dead if it has no works. (James 2:17.) Grieving needs the inspiration and power from God. God promises to reach out to us the more we let our faith guide us. We must carefully ease ourselves back to living in joy. Our loved one is enjoying greater life. This faith is the reason to smile and know that in faith, love, and grace, we will go on. We can help God do the work through other people such as a therapist who shares our faith.

Increasing our prayer time relieves the suffering. The veil between earth and heaven will become close when we experience death. Connecting with God will connect us to our loved one. Connect to God each day. Make prayer your habit.

The thread that separates us from God is slender tied together with ropes of sand. In this place we are surrounded by love. Prayer persuades our mustard seed sized faith that when our dear ones die, neither they nor we are parted from you.

God uses each departed one as a magnet that attracts us to the next world. This habitual routine can be at any time day or night. Sit down and listen to what God is saying to you. I have written prayers to God in my journal. I can go back and read them at any time. I will see impossible mountains removed, acceptance of major changes, and new directions, people, and places to explore.

God has given me the privilege to travel the world. In places on each of the seven continents, I look for a rock that catches my eye. I pick the most attractive, colorful rocks and take them to my home. The Bible refers to God as our rock. I write on the rock with a dark black pen the name of the place I found the rock and

I place the date on it as a reminder of a sacred place and moment in time.

My joy and pleasure have come from seeing mountains moved as I gather wisdom and information for the benefit of those on the healing journey.

I love fresh tomatoes. A person with a gift of growing can enjoy 100 tomatoes with a start of just one small dried seed. Those seeds certainly do not look like tomato plants. That seed has no taste. Farmers and gardeners plant these little seeds in fertile ground. Growers will water it. They let the sun's heat shine on the plants. With patience and time, we enjoy our grown tomatoes or those of our neighbors. Store bought tomatoes do not taste as delicious. Who does not enjoy a tomato sandwich? A fresh tomato on a hamburger enhances the taste. Mountains are moved and tomatoes begin with a tiny seed.

Nothing is impossible. Weed out all those negative thoughts. Watch the mountain move. Be in the process of positive changes. Create a meaningful new career. Experience the love. Organize yourself and the resources. Appreciate what you are doing. Affirm your ability to bring the highest good.

Think about the miraculous mystery of growing tomatoes.

"Even if the mountains are removed and the hills displaced, my devotion will not be removed from you, nor will my covenant of friendship be displaced says the

Lord, the one who has compassion on you." (Isaiah 54: 10)

Chapter Twelve
Healing Completely and Forever

We are responsible for how we live our lives. Our thoughts create our futures. We create illness in our body. We kill ourselves. Releasing resentment can cure cancer. Releasing the past and forgiving everyone who has hurt us are keys to living in God's joy.

My other brother is Edward W. McReynolds, M.D. We were discussing his medical career. As we spoke of our various ailments, we thought about the hereditary factor. Illnesses and conditions of the human body come with the wrong living of preceding generations. Our bodies resist disease. That resistance depends on the quality of our living. Our physical lives and our mental and spiritual lives depend on our obedience to the laws and commands of God.

Healing always involves getting our life and soul in order. That is a mountain moving task. Skillful and fatiguing efforts are required bore there is any improvement in health. We must follow our physician's advice. We face new difficulties. With help we can face the future with confidence. Healing involves facing decisions such as retirement or resignation simply and calmly. The physical body may not have a complete cure. However, with help we can experience forgiveness and inner healing of our souls.

A part of my ministry has been serving as a psychotherapist. The word comes from the Greek meaning "healing of the soul." I realized the possibilities for healing in my psychology of religion classes with Dr. John Davidson at Baylor University. In 2000, I received a Doctor of Psychology degree through the University of Oxford. This training enabled me to share my joy as a psychiatric therapist at the Lincoln Regional Center as well as other places with mental health issues. I told clients that

I was a joyologist. My skills created miracles in the lives of some who had been written off and rejected. Some lacked joy and lived lives of despair and hopelessness.

In my retirement years, I have trained to serve as a life coach. I have found coaching to be less taxing. I help clients by asking pointed questions to help them solve their own stated problems. As I stimulate their therapy, they do most of the work. In my understanding, there will be no negative emotions in heaven such as guilt, anger, anxiety, or fear. Scripture indicates that there

is only the joy of the Lord. David and those in the Next Place will experience healing that is forever.

Healing people demands that doctors and pastors and therapists give some time for self-healing meditation. If healers can no longer find time for prayer and the inner life, cannot bring the souls of humankind into the spiritual climate or environment necessary.

In Jewish theology body, mind, and spirit are in unity. The life we live inside the body matches with the life lived inside the mind, and the life lived in the spirit. Spirit life concerns the personal relationship of human beings with God. The healing of the spirit or soul happens only when one is face to face with God. Humans are not a collection of separate pieces as the Greeks believed.

When we are born, we begin our earthly journey in unity. There is no definition of the mind except in relation to the body in a unity. People who live with mental illness are not threats to society. Most of them are gentle, kind, intuitive, crushed by the struggle to live or to make their own living. Most feel useless and inferior. They have no faith in themselves or in God.

To become a success in the American economy, one must do the standardized obligation to be speedy and shrewd is more desired than the quality of work. One is required to sacrifice his family time for his passion for work. Only financial return counts. Most of that return goes to owners or CEOs. Workers make only one per cent of what the executives make. Fatal consequences result from the preference given to quantity as opposed to quality. Eventually, these slaves become ill, misfits, unhappy, and unproductive. Nothing is sadder than a child of God who is physically alive, but their lives mirror permanent death. Healing involves listening to those who are experienced in living. I have found expressions of happiness and shared times of joy in prisons, hospitals, nursing homes and assisted living centers. One of my realizations was that a healing healing was not just who lived the longest, but who had lived and radiated joy most of the years of life. When death is an imminent reality, the expectation is that these folks could share what has really mattered. During my own ministry, I sang and preached in places where I came to know and love those who lived there. My focus on purpose has now been refined and then refocused. Over and over, I re-dedicated myself to the commitment to proactively seek joy in my life by choosing it rather than waiting for it to happen. I have come to a better understanding of death. I am now more prepared to live and to be healed forever. My own sanctification (the word for eternal healing used by the Methodists) during the aging process came as a result of being surrounded by the spirit of my brother and others as they departed as beings healed completely and forever. Healing means departing after having lived a good life, with few regrets. Death is the final healing. Heaven is our hope for a perfected body and our complete healing. Our essence and unique personalities will continue after death. We are given a temporary tent for living. Paul envisioned the joy in heaven when he again met these whom he had the privilege to lead into the joy of salvation.

Our mourning will not continue. As our time on earth gets shorter, bodies come to wasting and disintegration. Weakness, pain, and hopelessness come with living in an imperfect world. We are assured of perfect healing. Instead of our dark nights of negativity and fear, there is light beaming from the face of God. Our healing transforms us to be like Christ Jesus, and we will become more and more like Jesus.

John Wesley experienced his death at the age of 88. Beginning his ministry at age 35, he lived more than 50 years establishing the Methodist faith. After his tireless days of preaching nearly 40,000 sermons or more than 800 each year despite the limitations of having to walk for miles or to travel on a horse's back.

During death in his own room on City Road in London, we had a tranquil acceptance of the inevitable. In his last days, he slept much and spoke little.

At times a flickering flame and his inner joy glowed with its old intensity.

Just before Wesley died, he burst into singing. He then lay back in exhaustion. When weakness overcame him, he miraculously opened wide his eyes and said words that became the strength of all in the worldwide Methodist church,

"The best of all is, God is with us."

In 2020, we celebrate the 300th anniversary of the Christmas hymn, "Joy to the World." During my annual Christmas Conferences, we sing this hymn with delight and enthusiasm.

"Joy to the world, the Lord is come! Let earth receive her King; let every heart prepare him room, and heaven and nature sing, and heaven and nature sing. "Joy to the World, the Savior reigns! Let all their songs employ; while fields and floods, rocks, hills, and plains repeat the sounding joy.

"He rules the world with truth and grace, and makes the nations prove the glories of his righteousness, and wonders of his love." Isaac Watts wrote the healing and assuring words. George Handel arranged the music in 1741. Living life to the fullest in the days granted us without the fear of death is the theme in the words of Friedrich Schilling called "Ode to Joy."

"Joy is called the strong motivation in eternal nature."

Joy, joy moves the wheels in the universe time machine. Flower it calls forth from their buds, suns from the firmament. Spheres it moves far out in space where our telescopes cannot reach. Joyful, as His suns are flying across the firmament's splendid design, run brothers, run your race, joyful as a hero going to conquest." At this stage of my life, I am rejoicing. I joy more than ever in my work. I am not trying to escape by focusing only of the past. Writing, coaching, preaching, teaching, and continuing scrapbooking. I resonate to the experience of Claudio Arrau after nearly 70 years at the piano: Now I play with more joy and abandon and confidence and discipline than I ever have before.

I enjoy people. With God, I absolutely delight in them. I find in my friends, who are at many stages of their ministry from beginning as a pastor fresh out of seminary to those into 20 years of experience, to my retiree buddies in a community of openness, a community of acceptance, a community that supports me without feeling uncomfortable or strangling me. They never cease to inspire me with their courage and faith. They delight me with their warmth and wit.

They keep from becoming unbalanced with their practical wisdom.

Speaking with college students, sharing baccalaureates with high school youth, speaking in reform institutions are my links to youthful vitality, ties to forces of growth in myself and in the world, the forces that keep me creative. I feel a deep and abiding gratitude to God for my life, for every moment I lived. I am ready to depart. I have treasures of joy and miracles for my lifetime.

The final note of the music in our life journey is joy.

During my years of ministry, I have prayed for thousands to be healed. Some recovered.

Some did not. The Bible has many stories about Jesus' healing people. James wrote that the prayer of faith will heal the sick. Reading James is a springboard for us to contemplate healing.

Inside our bodies are amazing healing powers. We become weak and fatigued with a virus.

The immune system attacks the virus. After a week or maybe more, we become well. After a hard fall, we break our arm or leg. A physician resets it and puts it into a cast. The body heals and mends the bone. Still God is involved in the process. God is a constant source of healing energy. Constant bitterness and stress can compromise our immune system causing illness.

Prayer and focusing on God produces inner peace to instill hope in a higher power to heal.

Being isolated from others and feeling alone can bring on more suffering. We are urged to connect to people who are ill. We become a connecting bond with healing power in the love we share.

Modern medicine should never be slighted. When my body could not conquer my blood clots and pneumonia.

Antibiotics helped. God's healing power works through a new drug or in the hands of a skillful surgeon.

Healing is always a mystifying miracle. "You do not know what tomorrow will bring. What is your life? For you are a mist that appears for a little while, and then vanishes away." (James 4: 14) The body does an incredible job of mending itself. Modern medicine plays a critical role. Humans will not overcome every illness. The last one, will be the last one.

Sometimes miracles happen. The cancer that doctors said would never be cured suddenly vanishes. As the illness retreats, the miracle defies any explanation.

Those who benefit from a mystifying miracle do not live forever. The miracle is in the inexplicable reprieve.

Healing brings a remarkable transformation. We focus on others. We can experience one more new birth, one more family wedding, one more college graduation, one more birthday, or one more destination to visit. Healing does not always mean a cure, a physical healing. Healing comes into the depths of the soul. With this we become at peace with dying. Helpless and weak, we may never from a sick bed, but we believe we will receive healing in the eternal realm of God. God's love never stops at our death. Henri Nouwen said just before his death, "When we reach beyond our fears to the One who loves us with a love that was there before we were born and will be there after we die, then oppression, persecution, and even death will be unable to take our freedom. Once we have come to the deep inner knowledge more of the heart than the mind, that we are born out of love, that every part of our being is deeply rooted in love, and that this love is our true Father and Mother, then, all forms of evil, illness, and death lose their final power over us."

Deep inside my mind I believe in the powerful connection between faith and healing. I embrace those promises in the Word of God that our story continues beyond death where we will be wrapped in the love of God forever.

Saint Francis of Assisi lived by the vision that joy was everywhere and forever.

Saint Francis, or Francisco di Pietro Giovanna di Benardone, lived from 1 181 to 1226. Millions have found strength from his little poetic song:

Lord, make me an instrument of thy peace.
Where there is hatred, let me sow love.
Where there is injury, pardon;
Where there is doubt, faith;
Where there is despair, hope;
Where there is darkness, light;
Where there is sadness, joy.

The second verse can be sung in juxtaposition to a time of prayer and mourning.

O divine Master, grant that I may not so much seek
To be consoled as to console,
To be understood as to understand,
To be loved as to love,
For it is in giving that we receive;
It is in pardoning that we are pardoned;

it is in dying to self that we are born to eternal life.

Imagine your daughter is a trained musician who teaches in Northern Ireland.

To begin the celebration of your life, she sings "Going Home" adapted from Antonia Dvorak's Symphony Number Nine, written by his pupil William Arms Fisher. Fisher lived from 1861 until his death in 1948. The music brings a hush. As she sings, she moves those attending the

funeral deep into their souls. Amy McReynolds stirs an outburst of feelings every time she sings. Imagine she is singing at your own loved one's funeral. You are moved not only by her talent, but by the words.

Going home, going home,
  I am going home
Quiet like, some still day
  I am going home
It's not far, just close by
  Through an open door

Work all done; care laid by
  Never fear no more
Mother's there expecting me
  Father's waiting too
Lots of faces gathered there
  All the friends I knew

I'm just going home
  No more fear, no more pain
No more stumbling by the way
  No more longing for the day

Joy Comes in the Mourning

Going to run no more
Morning star light way
Restless dreams all gone
Shadows gone, break of day
Life has just begun.

Notes about the Author

The Rev. Dr. James McReynolds has shared his spirituality and theology of joy in virtually every nation and territory of the world. As a pastor, licensed mental health practitioner, coach, conference and retreat leader, he has shared his care and counsel on grief in funeral sermons, hospice, and being there with mourning people before and after a death.

His education has included degrees from the University of Missouri School of Journalism, Vanderbilt University Divinity School, and Oxford University. This book was stimulated by the death of Jim's brother David McReynolds. Jim has prayed with countless people. He has shared how to help those who grieve in college and seminary classes, in sessions with lay leaders and pastors, nurses, any who need to recover joy.

Summarizing his faith, he says, "Being a good disciple is not a matter of credentials, But of following Jesus with a willing heart."

Once during a children's sermon, a little girl who had not been in a church, asked,

"Are you . . . Jesus?"

Bibliography

Asher, Alison. *Soaring in the Storm*. Seattle: Life Skills Press, 1998.

Bourgeault, Cynthia. *The Wisdom Jesus: Transforming Heart and Mind*. Boston: Shambhala, 2008.

Caughlin, Angela. *The Only Way Through: A Journey of Loss, Transformation, and Oneness*. Houston: Bright Sky Press, 2012.

Coffin, William Sloan. "Death More Friend Than Foe," *The Christian Ministry*, May 1985.

Frand Cherry. *The Grief Recovery Handbook*. Baltimore: Johns Hopkins, 2016.

Fumia, Molly. *Safe Passage: Words to Help the Grieving*. San Francisco: Conari Press, 2015.

Jeffers, Susan. *Feel the Fear and Do It Anyway*. New York: Ballantine, 2009

Kirvan, John. *God Hunger: The Mystic in All of Us*. South Bend: Sorin Books, 2008.

Lewis, C.S. *A Grief Observed*. Oxford: University Press, 2016 edition.

Lewis, C.S. *The Four Loves*. New York: Harper Collins, 2017.

Nouwen, Henry. *The Inner Voice of Love: A Journey Through Anguish to* Freedom, 1999.

Peale, Norman Vincent. *The Healing of Sorrow.* Pawling, New York: Inspiration Books, 1966.

Re, Cindee S. *Discovering Hope.* Waukesha, Wisconsin, 2018.

Richardson, Jan. *Circle of Grace: A Book of Blessings for the Seasons.* Orlando: Wanton Gospeller Press, 2015.

Smith, Harold. *On Grieving the Death of a Father.* Minneapolis: Augsburg, 1994.

Wallis, Charles. *The Funeral Encyclopedia.* New York: Harper and Brothers, 1963.

Westberg, Granger. *Good Grief.* Minneapolis: Fortress Press, 1971.